I, Justine

I, Justine

An Analog Memoir

Justine Ezarik

with C. L. Hargrave

Keywords
PRESS

ATRIA

New York • London • Toronto • Sydney • New Delhi

ATRIA BOOKS
An Imprint of Simon & Schuster, Inc.
1230 Avenue of the Americas
New York, NY 10020

First Keywords Press/**ATRIA** BOOKS hardcover edition June 2015

Keywords Press/**ATRIA** BOOKS and colophons are trademarks of Simon & Schuster, Inc.

For information about special discounts for bulk purchases, please contact Simon & Schuster Special Sales at 1-866-506-1949 or business@simonandschuster.com.

The Simon & Schuster Speakers Bureau can bring authors to your live event. For more information or to book an event contact the Simon & Schuster Speakers Bureau at 1-866-248-3049 or visit our website at www.simonspeakers.com.

Interior design by Dana Sloan
Jacket design by Mike Krisza
Key Caps is a trademark of Apple, Inc.
Emojis provided free by Emoji One

Manufactured in the United States of America

10 9 8 7 6 5 4 3 2 1

Library of Congress Cataloging-in-Publication Data is available.

ISBN 978-1-4767-9151-7
ISBN 978-1-4767-9152-4 (ebook)

To the Internet <3

CONTENTS

I, Justine

INTRODUCTION

SO, YOU COULD SAY IT ALL STARTED WITH A VISIT FROM THE MAILMAN.

It was a Saturday in August, uneventful except that I had received a package in the post: a white box with perforated sides, roughly the size of a legal pad and an inch or so thick. The package was clearly postmarked from AT&T; based on the bright blue Priority Mail sticker, it had cost the company more than seven dollars to ship.

I was new to AT&T, but the box threw me. As I unglued the flap, I contemplated briefly that this might be a warranty for my brand-new iPhone? Or maybe some kind of complimentary Apple accessory? Inside, however, was a thick set of pages. I thumbed through them quickly, not really understanding why I was suddenly holding in my hand a detailed record of every text message, data transfer, and file download I'd made since switching service providers. *Why in the world would they send me this?* I wondered. And then it hit me: This wasn't some welcome-to-the-family paperwork or a summary of AT&T member benefits. This was a phone bill.

It was three hundred double-sided pages.

It actually weighed a couple of pounds.

After the initial shock wore off—I mean, really, since when does a phone bill come in a box?!—I did what I had done nearly every day for the previous six months: I drove to my local coffee shop, Crazy Mocha, which had become my unofficial office (and virtually my only contact with people in the outside world). Then I set up my camera and filmed myself flipping through the bill—incredulously—page by page. I downloaded "Perfect Timing (This Morning)" by Orba Squara, the cheery acoustic-guitar-and-toy-piano melody made famous by its use in the first-ever iPhone ad campaign, and gave my minute-long video the (rather obvious) title "IPHONE BILL." Finally, I uploaded the finished product to several sites: my personal blog, the now-defunct video-sharing site Revver, YouTube, Myspace, and Yahoo. It wasn't the first video I'd ever posted online, and it certainly wouldn't be the last. I just didn't know then that *this* video would be the one to change the entire course of my life.

These days, going from obscurity to celebrity via the Internet isn't exactly unheard of, nor is it a particularly slow process. Justin Halpern of *Sh*t My Dad Says* fame snagged himself a book deal just two months after signing up for Twitter. #AlexfromTarget became a guest on *Ellen* inside of forty-eight hours. But the summer of 2007 was a different world, technologically (and culturally) speaking. Myspace was still the dominant social media site. (Facebook wouldn't surpass it for another twenty-one months; Instagram wouldn't launch for another three years.) "Viral" videos were still a relatively new, little-understood phenomenon. And the iPhone, now the most iconic smartphone in the world, had been on the market for only forty-three days. I'd had mine, purchased for me by a company called Technology Evangelist (because I had only two hundred dollars in my checking account and couldn't actually afford one—more on that later), for a little over a month.

Of course, the iPhone was immediately hailed as revolutionary. What became clear rather quickly, however, was that AT&T—the exclusive carrier of the newest, most advanced mobile device on the planet—was not: these guys had some seriously outdated billing policies. By early August, I'd heard about one or two unusually large statements; AT&T's decision to make (painstaking) itemization their default billing option was already getting play on some minor blogs and in the tech press. But I hadn't seen anything even approaching the colossal size of my bill, which—spread out on the little Formica table at the coffee shop—looked less like a phone bill and more like a Russian novel.

In the tech world, I've always been what you would call an *early adopter*, someone who signs up for new services and social media platforms as soon as they become available, long before they're actually popular. Such was the case with Twitter, which in those days was still very much a fledgling company. (Depending on which source you cite, there were only something like fifty thousand active users back then, compared to nearly 300 million today.) Since my account was linked to my phone, every tweet I sent (and received) was recorded by AT&T as a text message—in one month, with Twitter factored in, I'd racked up a log of texts in excess of thirty-five thousand.

So the length of the bill really wasn't surprising—what was surprising was that they printed the whole thing out and mailed it to me. I was upset about the obvious environmental implications. Which is why, at the end of the iPhone bill video, over a black screen, I had typed the words: *Use e-billing. Save a forest.*

To say it struck a nerve is perhaps a bit of an understatement.

Within twenty-four hours, the video had more than a hundred thousand views and I'd been interviewed for an article in *USA Today*: "How Many Trees Did Your iPhone Bill Kill?" Within two days, I was at two hundred thousand views and granting interviews to a handful of local Pittsburgh news stations. (I was such a n00b that I insisted on meeting this batch of reporters at Starbucks; I didn't want anyone to know where I actually lived. Also, during one on-camera interview, a bug flew directly into my eye. Take *two*.)

But it didn't stop there. I watched in disbelief as my inbox filled with hundreds of emails from literary agents, talent managers, publicists, and reporters and news producers from every major media company in the world. The video—and therefore my face—was splashed across the Yahoo, Myspace, and AOL home pages. The story, which had already evolved from a piece about the size of my phone bill to a piece about the popularity of the video I'd made in response to the size of my phone bill, was being covered in every important paper in the country, from the *New York Times* to the *Washington Post,* as well as a slew of international outfits, from India to Australia.

Justine Ezarik
@ijustine
Follow

I think it may be safe to say the iPhone bill video went "viral", if you will.

7:31am - 15 Aug 07

Within three days, I started a round of satellite interviews. I showed up at a small studio somewhere in Pittsburgh—and by "studio" I mean an empty room the size of a closet—where I was handed an earpiece and instructed to look into the camera while a chatty production assistant explained that this whole setup was a "live feed to New York."

"Oh, is that what's going on here?" I asked, completely without sarcasm. Amid the avalanche of media attention, I wasn't even sure what I was agreeing to; it wasn't until I was placing the earpiece in my ear that I started to realize just how crazy this whole thing was. A kind of mild panic began to set in.

Eight months earlier, I'd been at Macworld, the annual Apple trade show in San Francisco, to watch Steve Jobs unveil the iPhone to the public. Afterward, I was wandering around the floor of the Moscone Center, starry-eyed, when a reporter approached and asked to interview my friend Karen Nguyen and me. I guess I didn't hear her when she said she was with ABC. Also, I may have been a *tad* overexcited. Because when the reporter asked how long I'd been an Apple user, I responded, rather inelegantly: "Since I came out of my mom."

Pieces of that interview later aired on *Nightline*.

And *Good Morning America*.

As I recalled this from my chair in the little studio in Pittsburgh, I shuddered. Maybe I wasn't quite ready *for a prime-time live feed.*

Within ten days, I hit 3 million views, and the "300-page iPhone bill" had become a bona fide Internet meme. It would later spawn spoof videos and copycats; eventually, it earned its own Wikipedia entry. But if you go back and watch some of that early press coverage now, what jumps out, I think, is the comical disbelief on the part of some of those reporters. Because once we got past the size of the bill, none of them seemed quite able to understand how—or perhaps more to the point, *why*—anyone in their right mind would amass thirty-five thousand text messages. "Oh my goodness. That's a lot. . . . Do you have unlimited text messages?" asked one journalist from a local ABC affiliate, WTAE-TV. Glenn Beck, after wondering aloud if I "had legs" and asking the camera to pan backward to prove I wasn't "confined to a bed," asked me—on CNN prime time—if I had a life. When the interview ended, he politely told me I could "go back to tweetering."

I probably shouldn't have been surprised; it's easy to be dismissive—suspicious, even—in the face of new technology. Remember when no one—and by "no one" I mean *your parents*—could figure out the appeal of AOL Instant Messenger? Likewise, Twitter's 2006 launch was largely met with ambivalence. That's probably why so many of the interviews I gave had a flippant those-kids-and-their-rock-'n'-roll kind of tone. It's probably why, amid all that press attention, what virtually every one of those reporters missed was this: "IPHONE BILL" wasn't a random one-off. In fact, I'd long since quit my "real" job to focus on the Internet thing full-time. I'd been "iJustine" for five years already. And aside from blogging and vlogging and doing freelance graphic-design work to make ends meet, I was two and a half months into live-streaming my life—that is, broadcasting my every waking (and sleeping!) moment, 24/7, to the web, like a real-life *Truman Show* or an episode of *EDtv*.

Justine Ezarik @ijustine · 15 Aug 2007
On yahoo.com main page right now.. Kinda crazy.

★ 1

Jason DeRusha 🐦
@DeRushaJ
➕ Follow

@ijustine WCCO ran a story about you today. They said you were a man in Philly. I told them you were a woman. And on our air for iphone launch

9:30 PM - 15 Aug 2007

Becoming "Internet famous" was never my goal, but it also wasn't something that happened *to* me. I'd been cultivating an online following—without really understanding what I would eventually do with that following—for the better part of my adult life.

So, you could say it all started with a visit from the mailman, but you'd be wrong. That's only part of the story.

. . .

In the years since the "300-page iPhone bill" went viral, I've somehow managed to carve out an entire career blogging and making videos about technology, gadgets, and gaming. For my efforts, I've been called "the most influential person online." A few years ago, I ranked number six on *The Daily Beast*'s Digital Power Index. I've built a following of nearly 4 million subscribers across multiple YouTube channels, with total views approaching half a billion.

Trying to explain what exactly I do for a living, though, hasn't gotten a *whole* lot easier.

Granted, the third most popular video I've ever uploaded to the web—which has been viewed more than 7 million times—was a rant about a restaurant server who kept insisting on telling me about the daily specials when all I wanted was a cheeseburger. (It's called—wait for it—"I WANT A CHEESEBURGER!!!!!!!") The most popular video I've ever created—viewed more than 15 million times—was a spoof on the Black Eyed Peas hit "I Gotta Feeling." (Just so you know, I felt the need to apologize to will.i.am for this when I met him several years later.) A cursory glance at my main YouTube channel would reveal a slew of videos of me dancing (like a crazy person) in Apple Stores—and on an airplane!—across the country, a peek at the apps on my iPhone 6, and a series of ill-advised cooking demonstrations. Navigate on over and I'll show you how to make eggs, a homemade pizza, even a peanut-butter-and-jelly sandwich . . . *in a blender*. I guess what I'm saying is, if you've never heard of me (or you're over the age of twenty-five), you'd be forgiven for wondering, *Why does anyone watch this?!*—let alone an audience of 15 million.

There's been a lot of ink spilled in an attempt to explain the sudden rise of YouTube "stars," so I'm used to hearing people say things like "she just came out of nowhere." But the truth is that's a bit like calling a band that's been touring for ten years an "overnight success" because one of their songs finally managed to hit the charts—I've been blogging, often with nary a follower, since the late nineties; I was twelve when I built my first website. Likewise, some people have suggested that I stumbled across a kind of magic formula for creating "viral" content, but the heavy traffic many of my videos receive isn't *viral*, it's the result of building a loyal audience over the course of many, many years. ("IPHONE BILL" is one of the only truly viral videos I've ever created.) There's a small but vocal contingent of bloggers who are convinced that, based on my love of Apple products and what was once a stalker-like obsession with Steve Jobs, I'm some kind of covertly paid Palo Alto employee. (For the record: I have never received any kind of endorsement or compensation from Apple. Ever.) And in any conversation about social media, there are those inevitable references to "Generation Overshare," which is a polite euphemism for the idea that YouTubers are all sociopathic narcissists, that we're all deluded enough to believe the public genuinely cares about every little thing we do or say.

I can't speak for everyone on the Internet (and I have *absolutely* met one or two sociopathic narcissists in my time), but here's the thing about what I do for a living: it's really not about *me*.

You see, putting the bulk of your life online is a sometimes exciting, sometimes terrifying, borderline insane thing to do, and deep into my live-streaming experiment I started to bounce between two extremes: either I was so blasé about the whole thing that I'd ignore the webcam (and therefore the viewers) for hours on end, or so anxiety-ridden that I eschewed wearing tank tops for fear of having an on-camera nip slip. Slowly, however, I began to realize that it didn't matter what I was doing, people went right along having their own independent conversations in the chat room, on topics ranging from popular music to global politics to the minutiae of their daily lives. And really, isn't that kind of the point of the Internet? To bring people together? I just created a bunch of content about things *I* love, and posted it all in a place where like-minded individuals could meet up and connect *with each other*.

Running a YouTube channel is a bit like having a conversation—one that gets added to in installments, bit by bit, day after day. I've been having a conversation with my followers for at least seven years—some of my online friends have been with me since the early 2000s. Even before "IPHONE BILL" went viral, there was a group of people watching idly as I lived my life on the web. They were there on those morning drives to the coffee shop, watching as I tried to earn enough money to survive and learned the ins and outs of running a business. They were there when I received a three-hundred-page phone bill in a box, watching as I filmed and edited the experience in real time. They were there when I uploaded the video, watching as it exploded into a worldwide phenomenon. They've been there since the beginning, and they are a huge part of the reason I wanted to write this book.

If you've followed or friended me on any one of a dozen social media platforms, you already know that I wanted this to be a collaborative experience. I asked for your input about what anecdotes and inside information you wanted to read; you'll find those stories sprinkled throughout, every time you see one of these:

Some of you might even see your questions in the following pages!

. . .

After uploading nearly five thousand videos to the web, crisscrossing the country to speak at trade shows and tech conferences, and even dipping my toe into "acting" (I scored a cameo on *Law & Order: SVU* by tweeting the casting director—thanks, Jonathan!), I continue to be amazed and inspired by the limitless opportunities available to us all, online. For an antisocial kid from western Pennsylvania, the Internet became a magical place where I could connect with people who liked the same things I liked. After wandering into my first online chat room, I thought, *Finally, I have found my people*. On the Internet, I could actually enjoy just being me: a goofy, nerdy, Nintendo-playing, Pog-card-swapping girl who liked tech and games.

That's the great thing about the Internet: no matter what strange or atypical thing you're into, eventually you will find *your people*.

What's that you say? That sounds naive and silly? Well, have you ever heard of wikiFeet? For those of you who don't know, wikiFeet is the Internet's "collaborative celebrity feet website," otherwise known as the place for a bunch of lovable weirdos to celebrate and share their foot fetishes with the world. (Inexplicably, there are 612 photos of me—er, my feet—on this site.)

By the way, there are also people out there with sneeze fetishes. Did you know about this? Let me tell you, stumbling upon a compilation video featuring every on-camera sneeze you've ever, well, sneezed . . . it's a pretty weird feeling.

Beyond just finding a group of like-minded friends, though, the Internet has been, for me, a place of companionship (in virtual *and* in real life) and inspiration. Over the years, I've watched some of my online friends start their own blogs and YouTube channels; some have even catapulted to more "traditional" entertainment careers, launching successful comedy tours or writing and starring in their own TV shows. The Internet has allowed me to connect with people I would've had no hope of meeting from the confines of my rural hometown— people like Leo Laporte of *TechTV,* Justin Kan of Justin.tv, and Alex Lindsay of Pixel Corps—who were gracious (or crazy) enough to share some of their success with me.

There's a growing concern that social media platforms are only making us more antisocial, that technology is actually an impediment to honest human connection. But the Internet brought me out of my shell. It has put me in touch with some of the most influential and important people in my life. It has brought me solace and comfort in times of distress. And based on the remarkable amount of tweets and private messages I've received over the years, the Internet has allowed my experiences to bring comfort and solace to other people, too.

That's not to say it's always been a virtual bed of roses. I've been accused, frequently, of not being a "real" gamer. I've been described— in a reputable tech publication—as someone who "compensates" for her "unfunniness" with "bug-eyed, squealing enthusiasm." Like far too many people who choose to share pieces of their life online, I've received a colorful array of profanity-laced death threats.

The good has far outweighed the bad, though. It's possible that living my life online has even made me a better person—it's reminded me that what you see on the web is only a sliver of any one person's real life. In fact, I seriously considered titling this book *Tweets I Never Sent,* just as a reminder that no matter how much access you seemingly have to any one person online, you will never really know his or her whole story. Even when I was live-streaming, there were times when I said the camera battery had died, just so I could turn the thing off and catch a bit of a break from being iJustine. Even though I tweet anywhere from ten to fifty times a day, there have been moments when I chose not to share a particularly devastating piece of news I received at Christmastime, or to publicize that the tires were once stolen from my car while it was parked in my very own driveway, or to admit that a prank call led to a middle-of-the-night visit from the SWAT team, or to reveal that I once traveled to Hawaii with a boyfriend who didn't want to be on camera, leaving the Internet to believe that I was either (a) traveling, for some strange reason, entirely alone or (b) a closet lesbian.

Telling the whole story, for once, is the other reason I decided to write this book.

My life online has been a crazy, strange, amazing, and unpredictable journey—I have no idea where it will lead next; I'm still figuring this whole thing out a day at a time. But if there's anything I've learned so far, it's that there are worse things than being called a "bug-eyed, squealing" enthusiast.

I have been lucky enough to earn a living doing exactly what I love. I hope that, whatever it is that *you* love, you never let anyone make you feel weird about it. Don't be afraid to put yourself out there, to write or sing or draw or play video games or dance like a crazy person in an Apple Store. Do what makes you happy.

It's always worked for me.

And who knows? You might even build a career out of it.

xoxo

ij

THE GOLDEN RULE

THE DETAILS ARE FUZZY NOW, BUT I CAN TELL YOU THAT I WAS IN THE SIXTH GRADE, I was sitting in home ec class, and for some reason our teacher had decided to rearrange our seats—I ended up in a chair next to Steve, the class troublemaker. I don't know what started the fight. What I do know is that he kicked me. Hard. Under the desk. In the shin.

With no mind for the potential consequences—prompted only by sheer outrage—I kicked him back. He kicked me again. I kicked back. This continued on a little longer than perhaps was necessary, but there we were, surreptitiously kicking each other under the table, trying to avoid the watchful eye of our teacher. (Eventually, she did notice, of course, and ended up rearranging the seats yet again—we were on the verge of disrupting the entire class now, and there was also a huge likelihood that, allowed to keep going like that, we would have wound up seriously injuring each other.)

After school I was so upset about the fight that I immediately related the whole sordid story to my friend Natalie. As we sat at home, me rubbing my sore shin and Natalie listening to the gory details in wide-eyed disbelief, I suddenly had a wonderful idea. I fished out the school yearbook and flipped until I'd found Steve's photo. I scanned and printed a copy of it, drew devil horns, an evil-looking mustache, and scribbles all over his face, and sat down in front of my computer. Back then I was still using trial versions of programs like Photoshop and Dreamweaver—it's expensive software now, but it was exorbitantly priced then, so every thirty days I'd reformat my entire hard drive so I could re-up with the thirty-day trial. With my newly acquired coding skills—and the semi-pirated software—I set about creating what can only be described as a masterpiece: my very first website, about how much I disliked Steve (the actual name was "I Hate Steve," much to my current chagrin). I was still seething, and building a website seemed like the only way to get back at him.

Once I got over the initial flush of anger, though, something interesting happened: I was actually impressed—inspired, even—by what I had made. I had been teaching myself HTML for months—I had a Text-Edit file filled with lines of code, which I'd copy and paste into some of those early web editors, experimenting on the basis of trial and error—but I'd never actually built an entire site before. As I marveled at my handiwork, I actually felt motivated. That initial hate-driven burst of inspiration turned out to be just what I had needed, and it paved the way for other early and—let's just say it—*amazing* and tech-savvy sites: sites like IHateCows, in honor of the crazed heifers who frequently escaped from the neighbor's field to chase my sisters and me while we stood outside waiting for the school bus.

I grew up in a very small town in rural Pennsylvania, the kind of place where it was common to see someone riding a horse down the middle of the street, where goats and sheep and, yes, the occasional cow often wandered into my parents' yard. Shouts of "Call the neighbors!" would ring out through the house, and my dad would end up chasing the animals back to their rightful owners with his tractor. (My father has always taken excellent care of his grass, and I'm convinced the area farm animals were working collaboratively to get out and get at it. I believe this strange sort of upbringing also explains my enduring love of camouflage clothing.)

We did not live on a farm, per se, but we did raise chickens. It was generally my job, either as a chore or as an out-and-out punishment, to collect the eggs in the morning. If you've never collected chicken eggs before, a piece of advice: they're usually nestled deep within steaming piles of sawdust, wood shavings, and chicken poo. 🐣 💩 You've got to get in there and really *dig.* Suffice it to say, collecting eggs in the morning was disgusting. On the plus side, however, our chickens were both tame and well trained. Once you stepped out of the house and into the backyard, they'd waddle right over and bow their heads, beckoning for you to pet them. They were a lot like dogs in that way. We had a dog, too—an actual one—but the chickens didn't seem to know any better.

Aside from the petting and the egg laying, our chickens were also often the stars of the earliest Ezarik home movies. With the boxy camcorder resting atop my shoulder, I'd put pieces of feed on the keys of a little toy piano and encourage the chickens to pluck out a tune. My sister's pet guinea pig also featured prominently in some of these videos. (The poor thing ended up with a cancerous tumor the size of a tennis ball—but he was a trooper!) When I grew bored with my budding film career, I'd spend some time taking apart the VCR and trying, usually in vain, to put the thing back together again.

*My love of pigs started at an early age . . . a trip to the zoo
with my dad (old-school VHS camera in hand!) and sister
Breanne, circa 1988 in southwestern Pennsylvania.*

As is perhaps becoming obvious, I was kind of a weird kid.

I just knew, as far back as I can remember, that I was different. Making friends was always a bit of a challenge. I liked trading Pog and baseball cards, but none of the other girls my age were into that sort of thing. In lieu of going out, I spent hours and hours with my butt wedged into a too-small, child-sized rocking chair in front of the television, playing Super Mario Bros. and chomping on homemade venison salami (made from the spoils of my father's frequent hunting expeditions), which I called, affectionately, "Nintendo snacks." As with so many other shy, analytical, and tech-minded children, it's probably not surprising, then, that I fell in love, immediately, with my family's first home computer.

Our 1986-era Macintosh Plus was actually a gift from my mother's sister, Aunt Vicki. Between breeding sheepdogs and selling goat milk, my aunt had somehow managed to acquire a computer, teach herself how to use it, and hand it down to us within a remarkably short period of time. Vicki is the kind of wonderfully free spirit who can flit from odd job to odd job. She was always picking up to travel to some exotic destination, and I like to think I get some of my antiestablishment tendencies from her. It was Vicki who taught me a number of important life lessons, like "don't open the floppy drive when this little light is on" and "don't forget to save your game before shutting off the computer."

Though I have warm memories of printing out beautiful and elaborate banners celebrating just about anything I could think of to celebrate (using up reams and reams of that perforated, hole-punched paper in the process), of making elementary pixel art, and of teaching myself how to type, our Macintosh Plus was replaced pretty quickly by the much more advanced Apple Power Macintosh 6100/60. (A quick Google search tells me this model is currently selling for a scant hundred dollars on eBay.) You see, my Apple loyalty started early, for no reason other than the fact that my mother is a teacher, and grade schools back then seemed to be stocked almost exclusively with Apples—we bought this second computer with my mother's educator discount.

And therein lay the trouble: *all* of my friends—or at least my friends who had computers—had PCs. I didn't get why I couldn't use the same software or play the same games. At some point, several years later, I requested something called SoftWindows, which was supposed to emulate Windows for Mac, as my one and only birthday gift. Let me spare you the suspense by coming right out and saying: It did not work. At all. This ongoing problem with compatibility, however, would become a tidy little metaphor for my entire life.

Things started to change a little with the introduction of our first dial-up Internet connection. Once the earsplitting sound of the modem subsided, I navigated right on over to—where else?—Nintendo.com. Let me tell you, *this* was a revelation. Here were cheat codes and chat rooms and features about my favorite games! I could read all about what was coming next without having to wait by the mailbox for the next issue of *Nintendo Power* to be delivered! For the mid-nineties, Nintendo had some pretty awesome and heavily trafficked online forums, too. I remember they were modeled in the shape of a little house; you could ride a virtual elevator up and down to different floors, or catch some rays at the virtual swimming pool. I vividly remember my mother encouraging me to play outside more, to get some fresh air.

"But I'm outside right now, Mom!" I would tell her. "I'm in the swimming pool at Nintendo.com!"

When I found the Internet, I realized I didn't have to *go* anywhere to travel the world—I had everything I needed at my fingertips. I didn't have to be Justine from the middle of nowhere—I could be whoever and whatever I wanted. I chatted with strangers and invented elaborate backstories far more interesting than my own, and started to feel, for the first time, like I was part of some kind of community. And then, when I started to run out of things to do on Nintendo.com, I discovered a little button that revealed the HTML source code that powered the site. A strange and blinding array of angle brackets, tags, and commands popped up on my screen. I didn't know what it all meant, but I knew that somewhere in that tangle of words and numbers that looked like ancient hieroglyphs was the *thing* that made it all happen. I wanted to learn that language. I needed to understand how it all worked.

I frequented free web-hosting sites like GeoCities and Tripod and Angelfire; I copied lines of code from Nintendo.com, plugged them in via TextEdit, and saw what happened. I wrote my own garbled lines of invented code; when they failed to produce glittering graphics or sleek animation, I started over and tried something else. I discovered how to make a GIF in Fireworks. I hoarded those free-trial CDs for AOL and Photoshop and Dreamweaver. I figured out how to reprogram Kid Works, an intro-to-animation suite, so that if I typed the word *po* the computer would read—aloud, in that sort of post-apocalyptic, inflectionless monotone—the word *shit.* I cackled at my own cleverness. I demonstrated, to my slightly suspicious (and profanity-opposed) parents, all the reasons why this was both brilliant and *hilarious.*

I spent weeks typing out silly stories and creating accompanying animations, which I would unveil in elaborate show-and-tell format, as some kind of warped holiday entertainment. For Christmas, I asked only for RAM. I pushed both of those early computers to the limit of their capabilities; over time, I became my family's resident tech expert. And eventually, whenever someone in the neighborhood needed a website or an animation or help with their email account, someone would say—casually, without reverence—*Oh, Justine can do it*. In a town where (and at a time when) lots of people didn't even have web access, being able to actually build things on the Internet became a part of my identity, the thing that made me *me*.

Somewhere in the middle of all that, though, somewhere between discovering Nintendo.com and learning the ins and outs of HTML and figuring out that GIF is really pronounced "jif" (with a soft *j*) and adopting the moniker iJustine, was Steve, and that first website I built out of anger.

Steve never saw the site I created in his honor, but he would continue to be a pain in the ass throughout middle school and right on into high school. In ninth grade Spanish, he was once again moved to a nearby desk (because he'd been mercilessly teasing the girl who had been sitting in front of him). I held my breath and waited for him to say something awful to me, but he didn't. It occurred to me that perhaps I didn't need to hate him anymore. Perhaps he had matured a little. But before long the subject of dirt bikes came up, and he started rambling on and on about his irrational love for them.

"Oh, you're one of *those* people," I said, coldly. "I don't associate with people like that. You guys are *always* in trouble."

It was kind of a weird thing to say, and I didn't really mean it. I think I was probably just jealous—my mother never let my sisters and me ride dirt bikes, or do anything all that adventurous, frankly, for fear that we'd get hurt. But I knew by the stricken look on his face that I had cut Steve to the core.

A few years later, Steve's younger brother, Eddie, began dating my little sister Breanne. (For the record: Bre denies that they ever actually dated, despite the fact that they went to prom together.) And though I didn't find this out until much later, Steve spent the bulk of his junior year stranded at home because Eddie would take the truck they shared and drive it to my house to hang out with Bre. Can you imagine? Not being able to go anywhere because your younger brother, your flesh and blood, was hanging out at the Ezariks'? What a traitor.

A few years after that, long after I had started to build a web-based following, I got a late-night (probably alcohol-induced) Facebook friend request from my old nemesis Steve. That led to a conversation about our string of fights and what I'd always assumed was a mutual hatred of each other. But whereas the sixth-grade incident had always been foremost in my mind, it was the dirt bike comment that had lodged in Steve's memory. In fact, he'd been so insulted that he wrote a college paper about how mean I'd once been to him.

I'm not kidding. You can read part of it on the next page.

You might be pleased to know that Steve and I have since become good friends. He's a proud member of the United States Navy, as well as the safety and explosives expert for Pennsylvania's own Squatch Watch—a group of devoted Sasquatch hunters from our very own hometown. (Total members numbering four: me; my sisters, Breanne and Jenna; and Steve.) He's been in a number of my videos over the years, and he's an incredibly supportive friend, game for just about anything I can throw at him.

I was lucky: my "I Hate Steve" website went live in 1996, lasted about a day before I dismantled it, and was only ever viewed by two whole people—my friend Natalie and me. It's true that Steve gave me

Steve Moyer
Mr. Watkins
College Composition
5 April 2002

This is How We Role, Fool
————————————————————————

Riding a dirtbike is great fun and I have had fun doing it for a couple years now. I never saw a down side to it until one day. That day was the day I told Justine that I am a rider. Sure, before this people had made comments about it, but nothing quite gripped me the way that Justine, among others, viewed me now. Due to the fact that I ride, people hate me.

Let's go back a ways. Justine and I have been best friends since as long as I can remember. We never fought, or argued, or even disagreed on anything, no matter what the subject. But that was all about to come to a very abrupt halt.

The two of us were in Mr. Fields' eighth period class talking. This is when it started. I don't remember how I got started on the topic or why for that matter, but it forever changed the friendship between Justine and me. All I said was, "I can't wait to get home, so I can ride." Justine cast a quizzical glance in my direction. "Ride what?" she inquired. "My dirtbike," I responded. This is when things took a turn for the worse. "Oh, you're one of 'them,'" Justine said as she looked in the other direction. With a puzzled look on my face I asked, "Jigga what?" As she turned back, she explained that some so-called "dirtballs" on her bus sit by her and dirtbikes are the only thing that they talk about. These people annoyed Justine to the point where she could not bring herself to associate with anyone like them. With that she walked away and out of my life for good.

the motivation I needed—I'll always be thankful for that. But he also taught me, whether he intended to or not, one of the most important lessons of my life: be kind—even (perhaps *especially*) on the Internet.

Besides, you just never know when you're going to need a safety instructor for your Sasquatch-hunting squad.

BLOND (LACK OF) AMBITION

WE WERE IN KINDERGARTEN, CELEBRATING SOME KIND OF EARLY-CHILDHOOD VERSION OF CAREER DAY, AND OUR TEACHER WAS GOING AROUND THE ROOM, ASKING EACH STUDENT THAT AGE-OLD QUESTION: WHAT DO YOU WANT TO BE WHEN YOU GROW UP? The answers, up to that point, had all been fairly typical: a firefighter, a cowboy, a princess, the president. When the teacher got to my friend CJ—whose mom was best friends with my mom (his family had three boys, mine had three girls; it was all very *Brady Bunch*)—he stood up and announced proudly that he wanted to be a cop. When the teacher got to me, I stood up and announced proudly: "I want to be a chef at Bob Evans."

There was a fair amount of subtle head shaking and a fleeting look of concern from the teacher. A chef at Bob Evans? That was . . . well, let's just say it was a pretty random thing to want to be.

It was an especially ironic answer because I cannot now, nor have I ever been able to, cook. (Did you forget about the part where I said I once made a peanut-butter-and-jelly sandwich in the blender?) In my defense, though, I had to say *something*. And I really liked the food at Bob Evans (it's a chain of down-home, country-style restaurants, if you're not familiar); we usually went there on Sundays after church. Mostly, I just didn't have a better answer. Whenever anyone asked me what I wanted to be when I grew up, I usually froze. Or shrugged. Figuring out what I was going to do with my life—or worse, how I was going to make money at it—just wasn't something I was ever thinking (or, evidently, worried) about.

*Here's CJ, probably practicing some kind of
police takedown maneuver on me.*

My lack of career ambition might have been fine if I had been a more conscientious student—but sometime in the middle of third grade, my mother discovered that I was basically BSing my way through school. We had these workbooks filled with simple exercises and wide-rule spaces for writing in the answers, and it was nothing more than a bunch of busywork. I'd been *doing* the work—I was perfectly caught up in all of my classes—it's just that the handwriting I'd been employing was somewhere between out-and-out nonsense and a kind of invented shorthand. I mean, I could read back what I had written, sort of, so long as I squinted one eye closed and strained really hard. When my mother finally clamped her eyes on one of those scribble-filled workbooks, however, she decided it was probably time to go in and speak with my teacher.

My teacher explained to my mother, delicately and slowly, that she thought the scribbles were perhaps all I was capable of, that they were representative of the best I could do.

"THIS IS NOT THE BEST SHE CAN DO!" my mother practically screamed at her, waving the workbook around for emphasis. "She is pulling one over on you. Believe me, this is *not* her best work."

And to prove it, my mother carted that same workbook right back home and sat me down for what amounted to two or three hours a night, five or six days a week, until I had painstakingly rewritten what I had previously chicken-scratched my way through. We're talking months and months of work here, the equivalent of an entire half year of school.

Standardized testing did not go much better. Somewhere along the way, I determined that I was "great at guessing," and usually Christmas-tree'd my way through all those Scantron answer sheets. It's not that the lessons were ever over my head or that I couldn't handle the workload, mind you; I just had difficulty paying attention (something I still struggle with). I'd get bored easily. To avoid fidgeting too much, I'd sometimes take apart my watch or my calculator and attempt to put it back together again. Looking back on it now, I think I had (have) a mild case of undiagnosed ADHD. At the time, though, all I knew was that I didn't like school. What I liked were computers. So, from elementary on up, I did the bare minimum, studying just enough to get the grades that wouldn't get me in trouble.

Most of the time.

My mother and I worked out a deal (and by "deal" I mean that she set the ground rules and I attempted to follow them): I had to maintain at least a B in each of my classes. Anything less than a B and I would be grounded—no computer, Nintendo, Super Nintendo, N64, Dreamcast, Game Boy, or Game Gear—for the remainder of that nine-week grading period. Never one to be deterred, however, I soon found a convenient way around that.

My friend Zack had a little Sony VAIO laptop that he let me borrow when I explained to him one afternoon that I had been grounded—*again*. I hid this from my parents, of course, but as soon as my mom left the house to drive my sisters to gymnastics or softball or some other extracurricular activity, I'd pull it out and get online. For a while, I was able to get away with this. Unfortunately, we still had dial-up—so when my mom called the house one day, got a busy signal, and realized I was on the Internet (I certainly wasn't talking on the phone—I hated talking on the phone, and she knew that), I wound up in more trouble than I'd been in in the first place.

She wised up quickly. Not only did she make me return the laptop, she started taking the computer keyboard with her whenever she left the house. She just didn't know that I had a spare keyboard (and a mouse) hidden upstairs in my room. I'd wait for her to leave, run downstairs and hook up my extra equipment, play around until I heard the sound of the garage door opening, and then I'd pack it all up and dash back to my room. That worked just fine for a while—until I got caught doing that, too.

Now my parents were serious. They confiscated my spare keyboard and my spare mouse and bought a rolltop desk with a lock—whenever they weren't using the 6100/60, they'd just close up the desk, shutting the computer out of sight. So, I did what anyone in my situation would do: I learned how to pick locks. I'd wait for them to leave, creep downstairs, pick the lock, and plug my mouse into the computer (because, of course, I had a backup to my backup). I used a built-in Mac app called Key Caps, which allowed me to type using only the mouse—no need for a keyboard—letter by agonizing letter. I'd click out my messages and then copy and paste the text into a chat room or on ICQ (my instant messaging app of choice) or just surf the web for a while.

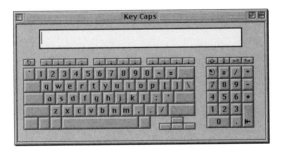

I guess what I'm saying here is, in addition to being a poor student, I was a bit of a troublemaker. And it only got worse with time. Because by high school, I had become an official member of the 1337 Crew.

"Leetspeak," or 1337speak, came out of 1980s hacker culture—it's a kind of Internet language where letters are liberally replaced with numbers (the *1* replaces the *L,* the *3* replaces the *e,* and so on). "Leet," meanwhile, comes from "elite," as in an elite-level hacker or gamer. Which is exactly what my computer-loving friends and I were pretending to be. We each had our own top-secret Internet handles—mine was xthree—which we used to communicate, undercover-style, via something called IRC (short for Internet Relay Chat), which was an early text-based chat system, basically a precursor to both AOL Instant Messenger and texting as we now know it. There were different channels (or threads) you could join, each denoted by a hashtag; ours was something like #L33TCR3W. And yes, IRC is where the now-ubiquitous hashtag trend comes from.

I chose the handle xthree (which I stuck with for years until eventually throwing it over in favor of iJustine—my xthree DeviantArt page is actually still active online) in part because it was gender neutral. At the time, most of the people I knew who were into tech, including the vast majority of the 1337 Crew, were boys. I was used to being "one of the guys." Sometimes it just seemed easier not to draw attention to the fact that I was actually *a girl*. Using the handle xthree, I could play video games without being judged and without feeling guilty whenever I beat my friends with Y chromosomes.

Plus, I liked being anonymous—on the Internet I was still pretending to be just about anyone other than Justine from the middle of nowhere. Most of the time, I was pretending to be Angelina Jolie in *Hackers,* fighting crime (and playing the occasional prank) with my blazing computer skills. The movie came out in 1995, when I was still in middle school, but it played a huge role in how my high school friends and I felt about ourselves. (The characters, after all, were high school kids, too.) Being able to code and program made us feel like part of a special (ahem, *elite*) kind of club. Watching the movie only reinforced the idea that what we were doing, what we were *able* to do, wasn't nerdy. It was cool.

True, "xthree" may not be as badass an alias as "Acid Burn," but as members of the 1337 Crew, we felt it was important to keep our identities hidden, since—just like Angelina Jolie and Jonny Lee Miller—we were doing all this highly secretive, illegal hacking stuff. (Note: we were not doing any illegal hacker stuff; we were playing video games.)

We even had T-shirts, which we made in graphic design class.

Did I mention that we were really, *really* cool?

When we weren't breaking into government databases (note: we did not break into any government databases) or uncovering dangerous plots to unleash destructive computer viruses on the world (note: we did not uncover any dangerous plots to unleash destructive computer viruses on the world; that is, in fact, the plot of *Hackers*), we were playing Unreal Tournament, Quake, or Counter-Strike during study hall, all of which had been covertly installed on the hidden directory of the school network by one of my classmates. (Everyone knew that by pressing Alt+Tab you could quickly switch between top-level windows, which we did whenever our teacher walked by, in the event that he might catch us playing.) When I wasn't playing video games in study hall, I was taking naps under my desk—I actually had a little pillow and blanket that I'd carry around with me; I'd finish my work and then crawl under there. My friends were kind enough to hide me from the teacher. (Seriously, how did I make it through high school?) And when I wasn't playing video games or napping, I was busy keeping up with my raging social life. You see, the 1337 Crew spent most of our free time at LAN parties.

We'd show up at someone's house with our massive CRT monitors and bulky CPUs and our equipment and our power cords, network them together, and play various FPS (first-person shooter) games—

Quake III Arena, Unreal Tournament—or, sometimes, Snood. We'd blast metal bands like Slayer, System of a Down, and Fear Factory, with some occasional Creed thrown in the mix (don't judge me). And while most of our peers were out drinking or (possibly) doing drugs, we were downing Mountain Dew and potato chips in order to stay up all night. Since I still had my Mac, one of my friends would usually let me play on his or her PC. But only after they had mercilessly teased me for a while, of course. I loved my Mac, but in the PC gaming world, having a Mac made me look like a n00b.

As a treat, we'd sometimes head to our local cybercafe, which was housed in a renovated church. There was some kind of restaurant there, too—I distinctly remember food (in particular, grilled cheese, which I'd proceed to get all over my keyboard) and pastries. You could also shop for a variety of firearms. Basically, it was a combination restaurant/gun store/cybercafe, and the cybercafe was in the basement. (Only in Pennsylvania.)

• • •

What's ironic about all this, and by "all this" I mean my lack of ambition and my fervent dislike of school, is that I had not only discovered what I was most passionate about in the world, I was already doing it. I had even been making money doing it. In lieu of getting an actual part-time job like most kids my age, I had been building simple websites for friends and neighbors (including Aunt Vicki, so she could sell her goat milk and sheepdogs online) for a couple of years. It just hadn't occurred to me yet that I might be able to build a career out of this.

It wasn't until later in high school, after I'd joined the 1337 Crew and started taking every computer class available—Basic, Visual Basic, C++, three years of computer math, Java, etc.—that I thought maybe I had finally found a viable professional future: at some point, I started telling everyone that I was going to become a computer programmer. Never mind the fact that I cared much more about front-end design—the way my programs *looked*—than about, you know, actual programming.

In the meantime, somewhere between attending LAN parties and taking computer classes and playing a whole lot of video games, I stumbled upon a second love: photography. I joined the yearbook staff, where it was my job both to take pictures and to lay out pages in Adobe InDesign. (This was also more or less the first time I'd ever worked with a digital camera; when I realized the thing could record mini-videos, I legit lost my mind.) It didn't take long before I decided to merge those two loves: I started a website called Daily Random Photo, where I'd post a funny, silly, inexplicably weird, or crazy pic every afternoon, sometime after I got home from school. (In those days, you had to build everything manually—code each page individually, upload each individual photo to the server, create each individual archive page—so it was yet another time-consuming hobby.)

I was lucky in that my friends were both supportive and interested in this new enterprise; Daily Random Photo became a kind of casual topic of conversation—*What's going to be on Justine's website today?*—among the people inside my group. Aside from my friends and acquaintances, though, I'd been spending loads of time on various Apple forums and Mac-enthusiast sites (especially spymac.com), searching for and chatting with people who loved Apple products as much as I did. My growing presence on *those* sites, it turns out, was further driving traffic to Daily Random Photo. The result was that I was averaging a couple hundred hits a day. Without even meaning to, I'd started creating content, building an audience, and harnessing the powers of social media. I didn't realize it then, but I was getting closer to the thing that would one day become my job.

With my growing love for tech and the responsibility of updating a daily website, it only made sense that I started saving money to purchase my very own computer. At the time, everyone else in high school was focused on buying a car, but I was so consumed by computers that when I turned sixteen I didn't even bother getting my license. (My friends all had cars and were usually nice enough to drive me wherever I needed or wanted to go, which was usually to one of their homes to play video games, anyway.) I tucked away the meager amount of money I'd made building websites for friends and neighbors. I scrimped and saved and pinched every penny I made for months and months and months. I squirreled away every cent of Christmas and birthday money. Near the beginning of senior year, my parents chipped in a little to help close the gap. And by the end of summer, I was able to buy a Power Mac G4. I loved it so much that I insisted on lugging the heavy tower and the bulky monitor into town, to the portrait studio, so I could pose with it in my senior class photo.

"Can't you just take a normal picture?" my mom asked, frustrated and sweating under the weight of the computer. (I didn't so much lug my computer to the portrait studio as ask my mom to lug it for me.)

"Mom, this *is* normal!" I yelled back.

I guess it only made sense that, a few months later, this girl who wore computer club T-shirts and took her senior photo with an elbow resting on a G4 monitor would be voted homecoming queen. 😮

and queen was held on
[...] game against Cornell.
[...]g dance was held on [...] the queen was Justine Ezarik. The
school cafeteria. [...] was held on September 22nd in the high

I know, right? It sounds crazy. I was someone who acted silly and hyperactive to hide my shy, antisocial tendencies and insecurities. I certainly wasn't a very popular person. I had no idea then (and still don't really know now) what people in high school even thought of me. Looking back, though, I think that was a blessing—it meant I didn't have to waste any time worrying about whether or not I was "cool." I self-identified as a nerd, but I was actually proud of the things I liked and I was never afraid to make a fool of myself. That's probably why I was generally friendly and approachable and talked to anyone and everyone in high school, not just my core friend group.

The news was a welcome surprise, followed immediately by the crushing realization that it meant I would actually have to *go* to homecoming, not to mention wear a dress. (I skipped out on my junior prom, opting instead to attend a kind of "anti-prom" with computers. My friends and I called it the LAN-ti Prom.)

I'd love to tell you a poignant and moving story now, about how going to the dance was a magical, romance-filled night, about how it brought me out of my shell, about how similar it was to that climactic scene from the hit movie *She's All That*—I mean, everybody always says that high school is supposed to be the "time of your life," and that homecoming and prom are events you'll never forget, right? Here's the thing about homecoming, though: I just can't tell you anything else, because I just don't remember. All I have left is that newspaper clipping. Oops.

. . .

As high school drew to a close, my parents remained concerned about my uncertain future. Subtle questions about what I wanted to be when I grew up had given way to not-so-subtle prodding on my mother's part: "Justine, you've got to figure this out." "Justine, you need to go to college." "Justine, what are you going to do with your life?"

By then, I knew programming was out, largely because Mr. Fields, my teacher in all those computer classes (the one who didn't mind so much if I napped under the desk, so long as I got my work done first, who pretended he didn't see us clicking Alt+Tab when we were pretending not to play Quake) had given me an important piece of advice.

Maybe the best piece of advice I had ever received, up to that point.

"Justine?" he'd said as he reviewed the recent work I'd completed for his class, a program I'd built from one of our workbook tutorials. "It *looks* really nice, but it really doesn't *work* all that well."

What he was saying was that I might want to focus on design rather than programming and coding. He was pointing out that I probably spent so much time on front-end design, in fact, because that's what I was *really* interested in. That's what I really wanted to do. It was just one more thing about myself that hadn't yet occurred to me: I could be a designer rather than a programmer.

As it happens, representatives from the Pittsburgh Technical Institute ended up coming to school to speak to prospective students a few weeks later. At PTI, you could study anything from graphic design to web development, from architectural drafting to criminal justice. The campus, not surprisingly, had tons and tons of computers. Then there was the clincher: at PTI, you could enroll in back-to-back semesters—no traditional winter or summer break—for two years straight, and then you'd be done.

"A degree in two years?" I said, wide-eyed with enthusiasm. "Um, *yeah*. I'm doing *that*."

That afternoon I went home and announced proudly that I would enroll at PTI, where I was planning on majoring in video production and multimedia technologies. No longer was I destined to be a chef at Bob Evans. (Not that they would've hired me, anyway. Seriously, *cannot cook*.)

My parents were, obviously, relieved.

SORT OF MAKING IT IN THE REAL WORLD

PITTSBURGH TECHNICAL INSTITUTE LIES JUST OUTSIDE ROBINSON TOWNSHIP, ABOUT TWELVE MILES WEST OF DOWNTOWN, ONLY FORTY MINUTES OR SO BY CAR FROM WHERE I GREW UP. Still, it was a major transition. I'd gone from a town in the middle of nowhere, a place where the streets often didn't get plowed for days after a heavy snowstorm (bonus: lots of time off from school), to an apartment from which it was possible to drive to a suburban shopping mall in minutes. I'd gone from living at home with my parents and two younger sisters to living all on my own (albeit with a couple of roommates). I'd brought my G4 with me, and—for the first time in my life—I was surrounded by Macs and Mac users.

There were PCs at PTI, too, of course, but with so many graphic-design and multimedia classes available, they were seriously outnumbered by Apples. For a Mac lover like me, this was *great*.

Classes, for the most part, were good: I was in a program that stretched from around 7 a.m. to 1 p.m., ostensibly leaving one ample time to work on various design or programming projects. My living situation, however, was a little awkward. Instead of traditional on-campus residence halls or dorms, PTI coordinates with several off-campus, non-university-affiliated apartment complexes in order to house the bulk of its students. I was paired with three other girls, and we shared a two-bedroom apartment. My suite

mates were nice enough, but four girls in one very small two-bedroom apartment made it pretty difficult to actually get work done.

I hung out there as little as possible, choosing to spend the bulk of my time in one of two ways:

First, I found employment with the Admissions Office, where it became my job to lead campus tours. For some reason, PTI was one of the first schools in the area (maybe even the state?) to own a Segway. I was required to ride one—inexplicably, the admissions staff thought this would be a real draw for prospective students—*and* to wear a protective helmet. I looked like a crazy person. More than one person asked me, with mock empathy, if something was wrong with me. "Is that why you have to ride this thing?"

"Um, no," I'd say, shaking my head ever so slightly. "This is just my job. But thanks."

Second—and I know this will come as a total shock—I spent a lot of my time online. By college, I had built a bit of a name for myself on a bunch of Apple forums. I was still using the relatively anonymous username xthree, but instead of making up funny back-stories and pretending to be someone else, like I had done as a kid, I was using the Internet to seek out people who liked the same things that I liked, and I was spending more and more time chatting with a growing circle of online friends. At the same time, I was all over spymac.com, searching not just for friends but also for news and updates about upcoming Apple products. In the fall of 2001, for example, photos and a description of the forthcoming "iWalk" went up on the site. The photos were later proven to be kind of a hoax, but it's generally thought that the rumors about the "iWalk" were based on the about-to-debut first-generation iPod. I mean, this was exciting stuff.

Speaking of the original iPod, I now had one, courtesy of my high school boyfriend. He had purchased it for my birthday from this web-site called eBay, which I actually had never heard of at the time. (By the way, do you remember the size of that FireWire port at the bottom of the first-generation iPod? It was like a brick.)

Anyway, as I began making more and more friends online, and sharing my love of Apple products with those friends, I slowly started to realize that I didn't want to be anonymous anymore. I wanted peo-ple to know, hey, this is stuff that I'm into. I didn't want to be xthree, x31337, x3, or anyone else but myself. Since I couldn't be "Justine"— that username had already been taken on virtually every major site—I became iJustine, in honor of the iPod and the iMac. I registered the domain sometime in 2002. It was as simple as that.

.   .   .

As freshman year bled into sophomore year, some interesting things started to happen in the tech world. For one thing, Apple Computer, Inc., was changing.

It's kind of ironic that I became such a die-hard Apple fan when I did—the nineties were a pretty troubling and traumatic time for the company. Following the now-famous ouster of Steve Jobs in 1985, the Macintosh operating system was allowed to grow more and more outdated; meanwhile, attempts to develop new platforms went nowhere, and Microsoft's already dominant share of the market just kept growing. By the time he eventually returned as interim CEO (in 1997), Jobs had to shake things up. Which he did, by making what would become one of the most important and impactful decisions of his career: He announced that Apple Computer, Inc., would no longer just be a computer company. The Mac would become a "digital hub"; Apple would begin designing an array of new and innovative gadgets to sync with it. The introduction (and success!) of the iPod—the first of those gadgets—marked a turning point for the company.

At the same time, with the rise of social media and the launch of Myspace, the Internet landscape was undergoing a major shift. Following in the footsteps of DeviantArt and Friendster, Myspace became one of the first sites to be driven almost entirely by user-created content. It's hard to imagine a world without social media now, but this was something none of us had really seen before: here was a ready-made platform to publicize your thoughts, your artwork or music, your interests, your very self. Myspace offered the music industry something it hadn't seen before, either: an easy way to quantify a fan base by tracking one's number of "friends." Once the music industry—first aspiring musicians, followed quickly by more established musicians and bands—signed on, everyone else jumped on the bandwagon, too. Just a month after its "official" launch, Myspace had 1 million users.

I didn't realize it then, but those two developments—the introduction of the iPod and the rise of social media—were about to have a major impact on my life, and it started when I stumbled across a website that allowed me to earn free Apple products through the magic of affiliate marketing. If I could get, say, ten people to sign up (read: enter their credit card number), the site would send me a free iPod. Since I loved iPods and I loved Apple, this seemed like a total no-brainer. I immediately started plastering photos of myself—posing awkwardly with an armload of iPods—all over Myspace. It didn't take long to become known informally as "the iPod girl." Without even putting that much effort into it, I ended up with something like six iPods and a free computer.

Now, please excuse me for a moment while I confirm that all those embarrassing photos have been properly removed from the web.

Oh God. They're still there.

Note to the ladies: seek professional assistance before attempting to shape your eyebrows for the first time. Ugh. I'll never get those years back. #itgetsbetter

Trying to score free iPods isn't the only reason I joined so many social media platforms, but it's part of the reason I started to build a rather large following. I joined sites like Myspace and Campus Hook, which was geared toward college students (this was more or less pre-Facebook). In fact, if you knew me at all between 2002 and 2004, I probably pressured you to join *something*. I was still running Daily Ran-

dom Photo, and I'd started blogging a little about tech and gadgets. And though I wouldn't have called it this at the time, I was also doing a fair amount of cross promotion (encouraging Myspace friends to follow me on Campus Hook, for example, and vice versa). The larger my following grew, the more I started meeting other Internet personalities with large followings, too.

Zach Klein 🐦
@zachklein

Met @ijustine tonight, astounded to learn she was an avid Campus Hook user, a social network the CV boys and I built in 2003.

1:40 AM - 6 Jun 2009

Steve Hofstetter was one of those people (not to mention one of my first online friends to cross over and become my friend IRL). You might know him—these days he's a successful comedian, as well as the host and executive producer of *Laughs* on Fox. Back then, though, he was an up-and-coming comedian, a funny blogger, and a writer for CollegeHumor. He had a sizable following, and I really liked reading his stuff, so when I came across his profile I decided to reach out and friend him. Because, why not?

Steve and I hit it off immediately, chatting about comedy and the Internet and comparing social media strategies. And then, somewhere along the way, I decided it would be a good idea to make a Myspace page pretending to be Ashton Kutcher.

Wait, let's back up a minute. Here's what really happened: I had a secondary Myspace page back then, which I used solely for testing purposes—whenever I decided to redesign my profile page, I'd experiment with the secondary page so I could see how the design looked before setting my own profile to public view. *The Butterfly Effect* had just come out, and I decided to use the movie poster as the default profile photo. Never in my wildest dreams did I think that people would even find it, let alone believe—for some inexplicable reason— that my dummy profile was the real Ashton Kutcher's.

I had been sharing some of the random messages I had received from Ashton's fans with Steve, but one day I thought it would be funny to actually *friend* Steve, posing as Ashton. I posted message after message on Steve's Myspace page, apologizing for missing his most recent show and asking when he would be back in California. Suddenly, hundreds of teenage girls started friending Steve on Myspace, too. Not long ago, Steve told me that his rise on social media began, at least in part, because I was (and am) a huge goofball.

It bears mentioning that impersonating someone online is a horrible, horrible idea, and it really wasn't my intention to do so (at least not originally). It's also extremely embarrassing to admit that I did this, especially in light of the fact that I would actually meet Ashton Kutcher many years later. But my intentions were innocent. Building a following wasn't about making money or seeking validation or boosting my ego; it wasn't some half-baked attempt to get "famous"—it was mostly about staving off boredom. (Granted, I liked the free iPods, too.) As I watched my friend count grow, though, I started to realize that there was really something to this Internet thing. I could see that there were opportunities online, even though I didn't have a clear sense for what those opportunities were, exactly.

And then, sometime in the beginning of my sophomore year, I met Desirée Cramer.

Dez was a freshman studying graphic design—we met through a mutual acquaintance and became friends almost instantly. Dez was funny and crazy and weird in all the same ways I was. We could chat about everything or nothing for hours on end. We both loved photography. We loved the same music. Sometimes we'd pick up and drive across the border to Ohio just to watch one of our favorite indie bands play.

By sophomore year, I had moved from my off-campus apartment into a large on-campus house. When I graduated, Dez took over my room, and I moved right to her couch. Technically, I was supposed to be back living at home with my parents for a while, but it was way more fun to stick around campus, hanging with Dez, crashing in her room or a friend's room or even on the floor most nights. I didn't yet know just how important my friendship with Dez would turn out to be.

By the time I graduated, Dez and I had already become regulars on the Pittsburgh indie music scene. We attended tons of local concerts, as often as four or five nights a week. We saw The Clarks and The Switch and School of Athens and The SpacePimps at our favorite hometown venues. I took moody photos of sweat-covered musicians and posted them to my Myspace and DeviantArt pages. Some of those bands even "hired" me to be their "official" photographer for the night. Of course, they didn't have the money to actually *pay* me, so they traded for my services with concert tickets and CDs. To make ends meet—because I'd never be able to afford a place of my own on a nonexistent salary—I went looking for a job at American Eagle.

Some of my "professional photography": (above) Guitarist Josh Sturm of Kairos.

(left) Neal Rosenblat and Johnny Naples from the Pittsburgh-based rock band School of Athens.

Since I was already a pro at getting people to sign up for iPods, I guess I figured that getting people to sign up for American Eagle credit cards would be no problem. The reality of working in retail, however, was considerably more complicated. Other than a brief stint giving campus tours, I'd never even had a job that required me to leave the house, let alone feel comfortable speaking with total strangers. I quickly realized that having to greet customers and talk up our in-store promotions was way outside my comfort zone. In fact, just walking into the store to get the job, past racks and racks of trendy, colorful clothing (none of which I owned at the time), I was so nervous I was practically shaking.

But it's funny how things work out. Within a few weeks, I realized I actually *liked* talking to people. I loved hearing all about the events people were shopping for, as well as helping customers find pieces that made them look and feel amazing. I realized I loved the company, too—from the carefree style of the clothes to the fact that it's head-quartered in Pittsburgh. Sometimes, while folding jeans late into the evening, hours after the store had closed, I'd find myself looking up at the models on the walls, wishing that could one day be me. (I still haven't graced the walls at AE, but I have had the chance to work with the company on some really fun digital projects in the years since.)

As it turns out, working at American Eagle didn't just help me hone my social skills; it was also the only reason I was able to join Facebook as early as I did. At the time, you still needed an approved college email address (with the .edu domain) to register for an account; for some reason, PTI didn't yet qualify. Lucky for me, our store manager had just entered graduate school—since she had two accounts, she offered to hand over the one affiliated with her undergraduate email address to me.

For the first several years of Facebook's existence, I would send out friend requests with this message attached: *Hey, this is Justine. Not Ashley Williams. I'm just using this account.* Only recently was I able to remove her name completely (to this day we still joke about *that time I was forced to be Ashley Williams*). How strange, though, to think that someone I met at a shopping mall, with whom I worked for only a couple of months, would still be in my life today, for no real reason other than the fact that she once lent me her email address? Well, that and the fact that she also happens to be a really cool, generous girl.

• • •

3 years ago
What was your job before you were a video blogger?

I needed to find myself a steady, full-time job, so I applied at a local Pittsburgh printing shop called Business Partners, where they needed someone to lay out and design flyers and booklets and brochures. Not more than a day or two after dropping off my résumé, I got a message on Myspace: "I think you just had an interview at my parents' place? I guess you're going to be working there now?"

It was from Brandon, someone I'd originally met online but whom I'd recently become friends with IRL. He attended a fair amount of concerts with Dez and me. He was also, unbeknownst to me, the son of the husband-and-wife team I'd just interviewed with. Crazy.

So, I got the job. Within a matter of months, Dez had her graphic design degree, and Business Partners was hiring again. Which is how Dez and I found ourselves sitting across from each other in the first of a series of offices we would work in together. We ate lunch at Panera every day. We were so broke that we'd empty our pockets and pool our change to afford an afternoon trip to Starbucks. We shared a little two-bedroom apartment in a redbrick building in a quiet suburb of Pittsburgh, populated mostly by elderly Polish people. (I only know this because Dez and I would sometimes sit outside and watch our neighbors file into the local Polish club for evening bingo.)

Life, for the most part, was good. I had a job—one that didn't pay much, it's true, but if I was able to cobble together enough quarters to spring for a five-dollar latte, I knew I was doing pretty okay. I had an apartment, which I lived in with my very best friend. I had a growing circle of online friends, too, as well as a respectable Internet following as iJustine. I was still taking pictures of Pittsburgh's local rock stars at night, still trolling for iPods and reading about Apple products and signing up for new social media platforms and websites in my free time.

And then one day, about a year or so after taking the job at Business Partners, a rather strange thing happened.

I was sitting in the copy shop when a customer I'd never seen before breezed through the door. He looked nothing like our usual clientele. He had a paper-thin mustache. He was kind of a flashy dresser. He was wearing a blingy gold watch that probably cost more than I made in a year.

I strolled up to the front of the store and collected the papers he wanted to have copied—flyers advertising a local doctor's office. *His* office, it turns out. It was easy to discern this, since his face was plastered all over them. Not once or twice, mind you, but multiple times. I quickly upsold him on both color printing and a heavier paper stock— "They'll look so much better," I said. As we were waiting for his copies to finish printing, I asked if there was anything else I could help him with. His beady eyes narrowed and focused on me.

"Do you know anyone who does video editing?" he asked.

"Actually, *I'm* a video editor . . . although, we don't work with video very much around here," I said, gesturing around the small shop.

He sort of rocked back on his heels and smirked. "Well, I'm hiring," he said. "If you come work for me, I'll double your salary."

I swear my eyes must have popped right out of my head. *Double my salary?! I don't care if this guy is out of his mind, I am so out of here,* I thought.

A week or so later, I went in for an interview, during which the man from the copy shop asked if I knew how to use an Avid. An Avid is a professional-grade video-editing system, the kind the pros use in feature film and television production. I had no idea how they worked.

"Absolutely," I lied. (I assumed—incorrectly, it turns out—that teaching myself to use an Avid would be no problem.)

So, I got that job, too. Which is how I came to work for a very, very shady chiropractor.

Dr. Rolex (not his real name) was the inventor of a device called the Back-o-Matic (not the product's real name, either). Supposedly, this amazing machine could gently realign a patient's spine by, uh, "tapping" the vertebrae back into place (thereby eliminating the need for all that awkward joint-popping and neck-cracking chiropractors are known for). Though he did treat the occasional patient, the bulk of Dr. Rolex's business was based on selling Back-o-Matics to chiropractors across the country. For the low, low price of one hundred thousand dollars, Dr. Rolex would sell you a Back-o-Matic, teach you how to use it, film you using it, and send you home with a package of pre-edited commercials you could air in your own hometown via public access television. My job was to edit those commercials. At least, that was the scope of my job on the day I was hired.

It became clear rather quickly that Dr. Rolex was a pretty weird dude. For one thing, I was expected to be in the office for sixty to eighty hours a week, though there wasn't nearly enough work to fill those hours—it didn't take me very long to splice the commercials together, after all, and only so many visiting doctors showed up in the office each week. Still, Dr. Rolex was obsessed with making his employees account for their whereabouts virtually every second of every day via wildly detailed time sheets. After being subjected to a fair amount of harassment for failing to turn in my time sheets, or for being too vague about my day-to-day activities, I started keeping ridiculously meticulous notes: At 1:42, I ate a turkey sandwich. At 3:07, I peed.

Before long, I started getting tasked with an array of odd side projects. One day, Dr. Rolex asked me to take some photographs of him to be used as head shots. Then he stood over my desk and barked out instructions on the proper way to Photoshop his hair. (He had a receding hairline, which he was clearly self-conscious about.) The next, he told me he was thinking about selling his house, so I was made to drive out to his home, photograph it, and put together a brochure for his real estate agent. He spent a lot of time talking about what a superior businessman he was, how everyone in his employ was lucky to work for him, how this was basically the best job any of us would ever have. He was bossy and egotistical. He was abusive and inappropriate. If you think I'm exaggerating, there is now a private Facebook support group for former employees. As time went on, it became apparent that Dr. Rolex wasn't just weird—he was crazy.

I was miserable. So, like the true friend I am, I brought Dez into this hellhole with me. I got her a job there, too.

There must have been fifty people working on the ground floor of the office complex, including Dr. Rolex, supported by a team of chiropractors, nurses, and assistants, but we worked in the basement. It was just me and Dez, AJ—a part-time video editor with his own production company, who eventually taught me how to use the Avid—and Darin, who was hired by Dr. Rolex more or less to babysit Dez and me. (I should point out that AJ and Darin were both wonderful, talented, and not at all crazy.)

Most days, I zipped through my editing work and then screwed around for the rest of the afternoon, counting down the seconds until it was finally time to go home. I surfed the web aimlessly. I checked my Myspace friend count obsessively. I juggled office supplies. Dez would hide the stylus from my Palm Treo around the office—that was usually good for another five minutes of distraction. We came up with more and more ridiculous things to write on our stupid time sheets.

Once, not long after some new office cabinetry was installed, I decided to see if I could fit inside one of the drawers. I squeezed myself inside and Dez slowly eased the drawer shut. I was still giggling when I heard the door to our office fly open.

"Good morning, team!" Dr. Rolex bellowed.

I immediately started sweating—both because it was really hot inside that tiny drawer and because I absolutely hate confrontation; this was not something I wanted to have to explain. Excuses started flying through my head. I decided that if Dez and Darin couldn't sti-fle their laughter—something neither of them was particularly good at doing, anyway—I'd just say that I was seeing if I could fit inside the drawer in order to properly assess how many DVDs we'd be able to store for future processing. *Yeah, perfect*, I thought. *That's exactly what I'll say. Brilliant!*

I could barely hear Dr. Rolex ask what Dez and Darin were laugh-ing at over the sound of my rapidly beating heart. Luckily, my cowork-ers were able to keep it together long enough to avoid ratting me out. I lived to work another day. And that was part of the problem: even with my best friend there with me—even with the distraction of our crazy antics—our jobs sucked. We were unmotivated. We were creatively sti-fled. We were depressed. Most of all, we were bored. Dez and I needed something to do. . . .

THE OATMEAL FACE, AND OTHER HEARTBREAKING WORKS OF STAGGERING GENIUS

ONE OF THE FIRST VIDEOS I EVER UPLOADED TO YOUTUBE WAS OF ME MICROWAVING AND EATING A BOWL OF INSTANT OATMEAL. Dez and I had our morning routine in those days: we'd arrive at the office early, usually before anyone else had come in; I'd check my email and various social media accounts; we'd compare schedules, see what videos we might have to shoot or edit that day; and then we'd hang out in the office kitchenette, chatting over Quaker Instant Oatmeal, which we ate out of Styrofoam bowls with plastic spoons. We did this pretty much every day, almost without exception. Until one day, I decided to make a video about it.

I was still running Daily Random Photo back then, so I was pretty comfortable posting stupid snapshots of myself online (to say nothing of those glorious promotional photos I took as "the iPod girl"). I had uploaded one or two short videos to Myspace, too—I have vague memories of doing a kind of Irish Riverdance, barefoot, in the stockroom at Business Partners. Once, not long after nearly getting caught hiding in a drawer, Dez and I spent the better part of an afternoon playing hide-and-seek inside and underneath the office furniture; I made a ten-second clip of myself climbing out of a cabinet, set to the theme from *Mission: Impossible*. Making a video about oatmeal, then, didn't seem all that weird, or even all that out of the ordinary. Besides, we were mind-numbingly, achingly bored. I would've done just about anything to entertain myself.

So, I placed the camera, along with an unopened packet of oatmeal, in a cabinet; I filmed myself opening the cabinet and grabbing the oatmeal. I repeated the process, but this time I put a plastic bird in the cabinet, too (which begs the question, why did we have a plastic bird just lying around the office?). I put the oatmeal in the microwave and aggressively poked all the buttons, feigning confusion, as if I didn't quite grasp how a microwave worked. I put the oatmeal inside a desk drawer; each time I opened the drawer I'd make a silly or crazy or just really weird face.

I pretended to maniacally stab the oatmeal with my spoon as if reenacting the shower scene from *Psycho*. Finally, I ate the oatmeal, staring straight into the camera virtually the entire time. I spliced together the clips on the Avid. I added a song. I posted it online. It was as simple, and as silly, as that.

Let's take some questions, shall we?

4 years ago
were you trippin when u made this?

Nope. As I think I've made pretty clear by now, days at the chiropractor's office were long and Dez and I were bored. I get questions like this all the time, though, which just goes to show you that "bored" and "high on psychedelic drugs" must look pretty similar on camera. For the record, I have never done drugs. Ever.

4 years ago
lol...so you thought "hey for my first video...it should be one of me...making oatmeal..."

This question implies that I didn't take my YouTube debut very seriously, and that would be correct. Then again, I didn't have much in the way of "examples" to choose from—YouTube had been around for less than a year (longer if you count several months of beta testing); the whole notion of user-generated content was still pretty new. There was no such thing as a YouTube celebrity. Hardly anyone was vlogging yet. The concept of being Internet famous didn't really exist. So, no, I didn't put a lot of stock in what people would think of my first-ever YouTube video. Frankly, I'm still shocked that so many people (467,915 views and counting!) have even seen it.

In fact, YouTube wasn't even my first stop when uploading videos to the web in those days. I preferred Myspace, Yahoo, my personal blog (tastyblogsnack.com, at the time), and—most important—Revver, which was one of the first and only video-sharing sites that allowed content creators to earn a share of the ad-generated revenue. Granted, my first few checks were pretty paltry: we're talking maybe two bucks. But the fact that I could earn money at all, just by posting silly videos I made with my best friend at work, was pretty awesome.

2 years ago
you microwaved your spoon...?

I *did* microwave my spoon, though not on purpose. In fact, in the uncut version of the video, you can clearly hear Desirée say, "I hope you like spoon with your oatmeal." I guess I was distracted?

4 years ago
she actually looked kinda slutty then

True, the black shrug over the blue tank top is, at best, a questionable fashion statement—I mean, it's very 2006. Then again, I *am* wearing pants. And a long-sleeved shirt. And flat, closed-toe shoes. And I'm in an office. Eating instant oatmeal. Maybe that's a pretty slutty thing to do, though? Who can say?

4 years ago
you used tap water for oatmeal???

Um, yes? How do *you* make oatmeal? With Evian?

I followed "The Oatmeal Project" up with "The Oatmeal Face," a forty-two-second video in which I pretended, zombie-eyed, to stir a phantom bowl of oatmeal, with my mouth open and my tongue hanging out. Near the end, I slid out of my blue office chair. It was set to "Lux Aeterna," that really haunting song from *Requiem for a Dream.*

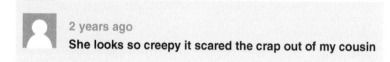

Yes, you are correct, I *do* look creepy. For some reason, a lot of my early videos were pretty dark and disturbing. I once made a video, shot at night, in which Dez and I walked up and down the sidewalk outside of Crazy Mocha, our favorite coffee shop, wearing superhero face masks. We found an abandoned sofa on the street, which we proceeded to sit on; we slowly turned our heads in unison toward the camera, then slowly turned our heads away. It was practically Kubrickian in its strangeness. Also, sorry for scaring your cousin.

Not long after posting the oatmeal videos, I asked Dez if she would hit me in the head with an apple. Why? I don't know. Enough with the questions, already.

We promo'd the video with a twenty-second teaser trailer, at the end of which I typed just one word: *Soon.* The full-length video features a lot of stalling on my part—"I'm trusting you!" I keep yelling at her, before crying out, "Just do it!!!"—spliced with shots of Dez menacingly tossing a Granny Smith in the air. Eventually, after a lot of prodding—and a lot of promises that, no, I would not be mad at her—Dez launched an apple at my head. I ran the throw in slo-mo.

She hit me in the ear, by the way. It was great.

Our next video—which, oddly, seems to be something of a fan favorite—was called "Have You Seen My Stylus?" As I mentioned earlier, I had a Palm Treo at the time, and I was constantly dropping, temporarily misplacing, or just out-and-out losing the stylus. Sometimes, Dez would find the stylus on the floor of the office and hide it from me for a while. One day I just turned to her and said, in a weird, crazy, creepy voice, "What did you do with my stylus?" At that point, filming a video about said stylus—in which I actually encouraged Dez to *lick* it—seemed like a pretty obvious next step.

It didn't take long to branch out and start filming videos outside the office in our off time. I was (and am) a huge fan of Mikey and Big Bob, two local DJs and the hosts of the Morning Freak Show on 96.1 KISS in Pittsburgh. They had a relatively large social media following, especially for the time. I remember feeling a little jealous that they had such fun, ridiculous jobs—these guys got paid a salary (with benefits, presumably) to be silly and stupid on the radio. I didn't see any reason why Dez and I couldn't do that. We were *already* doing that. We could

be silly and stupid, too! And that was pretty much my inspiration for donning a Teenage Mutant Ninja Turtles costume and running around the yard behind our apartment (to the *Ninja Turtles* theme song, obviously). Here's the craziest part of that whole video, though: you can clearly see my and Dez's apartment in the background. I didn't realize then how stupid—and how very unsafe—it was to make it so easy to track either one of us down via the Internet. It gives you an idea of just how naive I was. Imagine

how surreal it was, though, to see that Mikey and Big Bob actually commented on that video on their Myspace page.

1 year ago
How did Mommy Pack My Lunch come about?

It was the closest thing to stardom I'd ever encountered—not that Dez and I had stardom in mind. Our wildest dreams and ambitions were wrapped up in getting enough freelance work to quit our jobs at the chiropractor's office and go into business for ourselves. If we could show people what we were capable of—not so much the hiding in cabinets and throwing apples at each other, but filming, editing, building websites, and establishing a social media presence—they might hire us. With that goal in mind, we started our own website, followed quickly by a late-night podcast, called *Mommy Pack My Lunch* (or *MPML* for short; the name was based largely on nostalgia for the days when our mothers still packed our lunches for school).

It was, arguably, a strange idea: our podcasts were just as ridiculous as our videos. We envisioned *MPML* as some kind of pseudo–news station, but we weren't reporting on anything of substance so much as staying up way too late and taking calls from our friends to discuss . . . nothing important, it turns out. For no real reason, we filmed a lot at our local Walmart. One night we drove over there to buy some Clairol hair color after deciding to dye Dez's naturally blond hair brown (I played the role of Dez's hairdresser in the video, for which I donned a

The first Mommy Pack My Lunch *publicity
still . . . sooo professional.*

weird, floor-length, floral old-lady dress, naturally). Soon after that, we went back so I could walk up and down the empty aisles, pretending to talk on my cell phone, before taking a huge (staged) face-plant (which I actually repeated several times so we could shoot it from multiple angles). We were less Woodward and Bernstein and more *Laverne & Shirley*. We signed up for another Myspace account. I drove traffic from my iJustine accounts to our *MPML* site. We peaked at a couple hundred listeners for each podcast—not too shabby at the time.

Here's the thing, though: I knew, even then, that Dez wasn't really into this whole upload-crazy-videos-of-ourselves-on-the-Internet thing; at least, not in the same way that I was. She didn't want to be in the videos as much as *I* wanted her to be in the videos. I sometimes had to coach her (and by "coach" I mean pressure, prod, poke, and harass): *Say this. Now, say it again, but in a different voice. Be weirder. Be funnier. Hold the stylus higher. Actually, hold it in your other hand. Now lick it. Yes, you look great. Do it again. Okay, do it one more time.*

That's in no way a complaint or a criticism—Dez was not only my best friend, she was a great sport. But whereas I was increasingly serious about creating content and building a following online—registering domains right and left, signing up for more and more social media sites, taking more and more ridiculous photos, hatching more and more plans for silly videos we could make—she approached the project much more casually, as if it was just something fun we were doing together, as friends. Frankly, she didn't care as much as I did. And I was starting to care *a lot*.

I was spending hours and hours each week scouring the web for new ways to connect with people, as well as listening to podcasts (partly for my own entertainment and partly as a means of comparison to what *MPML* was doing). Dez and I aired most of our podcasts via TalkShoe, but I also frequented Odeo—a kind of podcasting platform-meets-aggregator. When the guys at Odeo announced a new venture called Twitter, I didn't just sign up; I more or less started live-tweeting my entire life. There weren't many of us tweeting back then; in fact, I kept seeing the same people pop up on my feed—I just didn't realize they were the *creators* of the site.

Justine Ezarik
@ijustine

+ Follow

Who is this Jack Dorsey character?

6:58 PM · 8 Feb 2007

I was also starting to film more and more videos on my own, without Dez. I headed back to Walmart for the launch of PlayStation 3 and made a four-minute video to summarize my thirty-plus-hour campout. Highlights include: spending the night in the Garden Center on a bed made from boxes of unassembled patio furniture; kicking a poor janitor out of the restroom around midnight so I could wash my face and brush my teeth in peace; and interviewing the ten people who managed to queue up in front me (I had no idea then that interviewing folks in line for major tech releases would become such a large part of my future).

And when I found out that something called PodCamp was coming to town, I immediately signed myself up for that, too.

PodCamp (my friends kept referring to it as "iPod Camp," no doubt envisioning some kind of weekend-long summer camp for Apple nerds . . . which, actually, is not *that* far off . . .) was a free, low-key tech conference for new-media enthusiasts. (The founders actually referred to it as an *un*conference to emphasize the informal, unorganized nature of the event.) Bloggers, podcasters, social networkers, and YouTubers—or anyone, really, who was remotely interested in the digital tech space—could sign up to learn new skills, network with one another, and hear talks from both amateurs and professionals working in the field. One of the professionals scheduled to speak that year was Alex Lindsay, a Pittsburgh native living in Silicon Valley.

It wouldn't be an exaggeration to say that Alex Lindsay is a rock star in the digital world. He's the founder of a media production company and training group called Pixel Corps, which teaches people skills like digital animation, photo editing and retouching, matte painting, lighting, and camera operation. He's also a former employee of Industrial Light & Magic, George Lucas's visual effects company, where he worked for several years on the animation for *Star Wars: Episode I; The Phantom Menace*. His company Pixel Corps is responsible for co-producing what I generally consider to be the greatest podcast of all time, *MacBreak* (dedicated entirely to Apple products—*hello*). And if that wasn't enough, Alex was a frequent guest star on *TechTV*.

When I was a kid, my grandma Grayce often babysat my sisters and me in the afternoons while our parents were still at work. My grandma has always been incredibly artistic and creative. She's an amateur painter, and she was usually encouraging my sisters and me to paint, or buying us pastels and charcoal pencils, or taking us with her on trips to the craft store. But she was super supportive of and interested in the creative things I could do with the computer, too, from those first pixel animations on the Macintosh Plus to the animated GIFs I made on the 6100/60. So, when we weren't painting or drawing, sometimes Grandma and I would curl up on the couch and watch my favorite shows on *TechTV*, starring experts like Chris Pirillo, Kevin Rose, and Leo Laporte. Instead of boy bands, I had been idolizing tech rock stars for years.

I showed up for the first day of PodCamp eager to learn. Alex's talk was first, and he focused on shooting with higher-end cameras and the finer points of green-screening. During his actual presentation, though, I could barely contain myself—I just started asking the guy breathless, rapid-fire questions about everything I had ever wanted to know about video production. I could tell that he was surprised by the sheer volume of questions I had, as well as confused as to why I kept bringing the conversation back to YouTube, but that he also recognized that this was stuff I genuinely, deeply cared about and was interested in; after his talk, we chatted for a while about our mutual love of Apple and technology and decided to keep in touch.

Imagine my surprise, though, when I discovered that befriending Alex Lindsay wasn't even the best part of the conference: I was blown away by the collective creativity and enthusiasm of the other attendees. Here was a whole host of people, all from my very own hometown, no less, who were excited about and committed to the same ideas and ideals that I was. I'd never before felt so at home within such a large group. Which may be why—on the night before the last day of PodCamp—I worked up the courage to book a room and give my *own* talk. (I wasn't kidding when I said this was a laid-back convention; just about anyone could speak if they wanted to.)

For my PodCamp debut, I decided to give a tutorial on using jumpcut.com, a website where you could upload, edit, and publish videos in real time. I'd been using the site to edit most of my content, but Jumpcut was yet another space for like-minded people to connect and chat with each other. I'd struck up an easy friendship with a user named Karen; only later would I discover that she was actually a Jumpcut employee. Through Karen Nguyen, I would eventually become friends with the entire Jumpcut crew.

I was pleased the turnout for my lesson ended up being pretty decent. I was even more pleased, though, to discover how diverse the group was: in my session alone, I spoke with a teenager, a dance instructor, a comic book illustrator, a schoolteacher, an actor, and other folks from all walks of life. I loved thinking about the different ways in which those people might put to use what I'd shown them. I didn't yet realize the ways in which PodCamp was going to have a major effect on my future, though. I didn't know then that signing up for the first-ever Pittsburgh PodCamp would change my life.

• • •

1 year ago
When did you realize you could "quit your day job" so to speak?

High off my "success" at PodCamp, meeting Alex Lindsay, and putting more and more original content online, I felt on the cusp of something. It was around that time that I realized I was going to have to quit my job with the chiropractor. I didn't have anything else in the way of full-time work lined up, and the residuals I was making from the web were still measly. But I was miserable. I didn't want to waste one more minute working somewhere I hated (never mind the fact that I was only twenty-two); I wanted to devote all my time to whatever it was I was trying to build or do or achieve via the web.

I discussed my decision with Dez, of course; she was supportive, although she wasn't willing to quit *her* job just yet. (I can't say I blame her.) Still, it took me a while to work up the nerve to break the news to Dr. Rolex. When I finally did, it was just as awful as I thought it would be: he actually told me I was worthless, I'd never find a better job, and I'd never amount to anything if I left. I knew he wasn't right—I knew he was a sad, egotistical 🐷 —but I'd never been spoken to like that before, and I left his office with tears streaming down my face. In spite of my embarrassment at being berated, I felt something else, though: relief. I wasn't going to have to take any more crap from that guy, or from anyone else, for that matter. *I'm going to make it on my own,* I thought. *Watch me.*

Of course, my parents were none too pleased. Dr. Rolex had meant it when he said he would double the salary I'd been making at Business Partners; my parents couldn't comprehend why I would throw away a steady, sizable paycheck. I promised them I would figure something out, told them that no amount of money in the world was worth being that miserable, but the little cash I had saved went quickly: I had to buy myself a laptop (I'd been using the computer at the office; my G4 was long gone by then). I was late with my rent a few times. I got pretty good at giving my landlord spur-of-the-moment excuses for why I hadn't yet paid. (*Oh! Can you believe it? My check got lost in the mail!* Or *I'm actually on my way*—said sneaking out to my car—*to the bank*—putting the key in the ignition—*right now! I'll be back soon*—and peeling out of the driveway.) Difficult as it was at the time, I wasn't deterred, though. I was determined.

It would take me quite a while to get back on my feet financially, but I heard rumors about Dr. Rolex over the years: there were some lawsuits, and his office building was eventually bulldozed. I don't know if he ever saw any of the videos that Dez and I filmed in his basement—I haven't laid eyes on him since walking out of his office on the day that I quit. All I know is that things apparently didn't work out so well for *him* in the end.

But as for me . . . I had a hunch they'd turn out all right.

AND NOW, FOR THE TALENT PORTION . . .

SO, NOW I WAS BROKE. And unemployed. But I was lucky: it didn't take very long to figure out what I was going to do next.

In my usual daily perusal of the Internet, I discovered that Yahoo was hosting a nationwide talent search. Over the course of six weeks, anyone from anywhere could upload as many as fifty videos of themselves, showcasing their "talents"—stand-up comedy, animation, performance art, whatever you were into, whatever you were good at. Yahoo was looking for the original "Web Celeb."

That sounded promising. But as I read through the press release, I started to get more and more excited: after a period of open voting, five finalists would be selected to compete in a series of video challenges, the last of which would be filmed and edited in New York City, and then shown in front of a panel of judges, including television personality Maria Sansone (now a coanchor on *Good Day LA*), the Ninja from AskANinja.com, and Tom Green.

That would have been enough right there: I *loved* Tom Green. This was late 2006, the post–*Road Trip,* post-MTV era in Green's long career;

he'd moved on by then to hosting *Tom Green Live!* (later called *Tom Green's House Tonight*), an Internet talk show filmed right in his own Hollywood Hills living room, and Tom Green had my kind of humor. He just did and said whatever he wanted and it always felt genuine and funny. He was something of an inspiration to me. The opportunity to actually meet him in person would be amazing.

Except it didn't stop there. I kept reading.

After the final videos were shown, the Internet would vote again and select a winner. The grand prize was fifty thousand dollars (OMG, fifty grand?! I'd be able to keep trying to figure out this Internet thing without having to get a "real" job!). Oh, and there was also a chance to star in your own show on Yahoo.

Over the next few weeks, I submitted a total of twenty-one videos, including the one of my adventures waiting in line for a PS3, "Have You Seen My Stylus?," and a video of me juggling with a stranger's cell phone in the parking lot of Walmart. (Seriously: Walmart. Crazy Mocha. The only places I saw other than the inside of my apartment after quitting my job with the chiropractor.) I held my breath for the next month or so, waiting to see if I'd be named a finalist.

Each week I'd tune in to the official online show, where the host, television personality Mayleen Ramey, would promote the contest; conduct random man-on-the-street-style interviews, asking people to show *their* talents; or showcase some of the videos that had been submitted thus far, spliced together with preliminary feedback from the panel of judges. I posted about the contest everywhere—Myspace, Twitter, my blog (tastyblogsnack.com), my xthree LiveJournal account, Facebook, Campus Hook; you name it, I posted, asking people to vote for me. On November 21, I launched my first official YouTube channel under the name iJustine, and asked people to vote for me there, too. A few days later, a "Happy Thanksgiving" video I'd filmed (in which I got into a virtual fight with a clip-art turkey) was featured prominently on the main page of the *Yahoo! Talent Show*; it was also named "Video of the Week" on a popular blog that provided news on and analysis of the video-sharing industry. I started to feel like maybe I had a chance at this thing. I allowed myself to wonder: Could I really make the cut?

On Monday, December 4, Yahoo made the official announcement via the Internet show. In no particular order, the finalists were:

- Rex Hermogino, a San Diego native whose original song "Love on the Internet" had gone viral (incidentally, *viral,* at the time, equated a hundred thousand views).
- Ben Grinnell, aka Awkward Rick, who conducted really, well, awkward (albeit hilarious) interviews while sporting unwashed, matted hair and wearing oversized glasses that slipped down his nose.
- Rob Ray and his parkour team, Renzhe Parkour.
- Stanley Sowa Jr., who made videos featuring hand-drawn stick-figure animation.

And . . . the *final* finalist . . . the only girl in the whole group (drum-roll, please) . . .

- Justine *Evarik,* who "sent in a lot of stuff about nothing" but who proved "that nothing could be a lot of fun."

That's not a typo, by the way—Mayleen totally said my name wrong. Maria Sansone said she liked me because I wasn't afraid to "act a fool." In the press release announcing the finalists, they described my "talent" as "variety show antics."

But who cares? I was in!! I was a finalist! I was going to New York and I was going to win!!

After screaming with excitement and jumping up and down for a while, the first thing I did was share the news with Dez. The second thing I did was beg her to come with me. I had submitted the videos under my own name, but there was no way I was going to New York without her. I wanted this to be something else we were doing together. Thankfully, she was just as supportive and up for it as ever.

The second phase of the competition, which we had to embark on right away, even before heading to New York, was the aforementioned series of video "challenges." Dez and I decided to film a weird skit about teleporting (via the magic of video editing), which we'd shoot primarily at our apartment and Primanti Brothers, a famous sandwich chain in Pittsburgh. The idea was that I'd "teleport" to Dez's house (even though we lived together—in the video you can clearly see our redbrick apartment building, the same one from the Ninja Turtles video), then we'd teleport to the restaurant. Dez would make it, no problem, but I'd have some trouble: teleporting, by mistake, to the parking lot, to a table full of middle-aged men, behind a large potted plant, on the hood of a car, to a stranger's house (while holding a random tiny dog), before finally appearing at our designated table by Dez's side.

That Saturday we started filming all the necessary clips at various locations in preparation for Sunday's deadline (incidentally, Yahoo didn't give us a lot of lead time). Things were going well. I was happy with the footage we'd shot thus far. And then tragedy struck.

We were headed to our next location, and we were in a hurry. We set the bulk of our equipment on the sidewalk to discuss next steps, and then we piled into our van and sped off. It wasn't until we were several blocks away that I realized: *we left all of the equipment on the sidewalk.* We'd been so rushed that we completely forgot to actually load it into the van.

When we circled back, it was already gone: two still cameras, two video cameras, lenses, mics, accessories, everything. Gone. The value of the equipment was more than ten thousand dollars. I felt my knees go weak. I thought I was going to break down and cry. Not only had we lost so much expensive equipment—which wasn't mine, which I had absolutely no way of replacing (I was unemployed; I didn't have anywhere near that kind of money in the bank)—but we were up against a punishing deadline. Within the next fifteen hours or so, we were going to have to somehow round up some more equipment, reshoot everything we'd already shot, edit the whole thing together, and send it off to the folks at Yahoo. Without that video, we were as good as eliminated from the competition before it had even really started.

Justine Ezarik 🐦
@ijustine

+⚫ Follow

I haven't updated in 24 hours. if anyone has an extra $10,000 I can borrow.. Thatd be great. Someone stole all of my video/photo equipment!

↩   ↻   ★   •••

1:43 PM - 3 Dec 2006

We scrambled. We called everyone we knew. We begged and we pleaded. And I found a couple of angels to save the day: Justin Kownacki agreed to lend us a camera. A Pittsburgh native, Justin is also the creator of *Something to Be Desired,* the first and longest-running original web series. Two more friends, Danny Yourd and Steve Hoover, let us borrow some additional equipment and shoot in their studio. Guess where I met Danny and Steve? On Myspace. These guys would go on to produce and direct, respectively, a documentary called *Blood Brother,* which won both the Grand Jury Prize and the Audience Award for U.S. Documentary at the 2013 Sundance Film Festival. I don't know if there's something in the water in Pittsburgh, or just something *that* incredible about the local online community, but there is nothing more amazing than seeing the heights your friends can reach when you're familiar with the place they started.

With help from my incredible tech friends, we were able to reshoot everything, edit the video, and send it off in time. Within just a few days, Dez and I would be in New York City, courtesy of Yahoo.

• • •

I'd never really been anywhere particularly exciting in my life. I'd traveled to North Carolina for vacation. I'd been to Florida a time or two. I was dying to go to San Francisco. I was aching to get out of Pittsburgh. But I certainly hadn't expected that my first trip to New York would be a kind of paid vacation, with my best friend, where I'd meet Tom Green, and maybe win a job hosting and producing my own Internet-based variety show.

The goal in New York was to shoot the pilot episode, but most of that trip is a blur to me now. We were teamed with a producer, given some equipment, and sent into the field. I ran around Manhattan for a while in a Superman costume. We edited the thing at Sony Music Studios in Midtown (and by "edited" I mean I had to hand off our footage to someone else, who did an okay job but who left a lot of my favorite clips out of the final cut—by that point, we were under insane time constraints, so there just wasn't time for any last-minute haggling). We went to Times Square and waved signs for the *Yahoo! Talent Show* in the air with a bunch of San-

You would think
hailing a cab would
be easier when
you're Superman . . .

Dez and me, posing
with some of our
fellow Yahoo! Talent
Show contestants in

tas, as some kind of promotional stunt (it was December). We loitered outside the *Good Morning America* studio with Tom Green. We visited the subterranean flagship Apple Store on Fifth Avenue, at the southeast corner of Central Park, where I was yelled at repeatedly for putting my hands on the famous aboveground glass cube.

I knew my online friends were rooting for me—including Karen from Jumpcut, who wrote about me on her personal blog. Actual excerpt: "I really really really like ijustine and I totally want her to win (though I have to admit her pilot video is weak)."

Side note: I sort of hated my pilot video, too.

But before I knew it, the moment was upon us. It was time for the big reveal.

We filed into the studio, met with the judges, took a bunch of group selfies (even though "selfie" wasn't a word yet), and then it was just a matter of watching all of the episodes and waiting to hear the results. I was so excited, and so unbelievably nervous. We had put so much work into this silly contest, hoping it would completely change the course of our lives. With no money and no job, I had no idea how else I might pay the bills piling up back home in Pittsburgh.

But I didn't win.

The grand prize went to Rex Hermogino, the "Love on the Internet" guy. I probably should have known things weren't looking too good for me when Tom Green called me "the Clay Aiken of the competition."

Justine Ezarik ✔
@ijustine

⁑ Follow

Good thing I like Google more than Yahoo.

↩ ↻ ★ •••

7:20 AM - 14 Dec 2006

In the early days of being iJustine, I often had to validate what exactly it was I was doing—the people closest to me were supportive (usually), albeit a little concerned. "We think it's funny and all, what you're doing," they would say, "but . . . is this a *job*? What are you actually going to do with your life? How are you going to survive?" The only response I ever gave my friends or family was to shrug. I just had an inkling that despite the apparent craziness of my life, despite the unconventional nature of my "career" aspirations, I was on to something.

I left the *Yahoo! Talent Show* with some bruises. The sting of not winning paled in comparison to the gut punch of reading so many negative comments about myself online. I hadn't been quite ready for the sheer *volume* of them; the exposure I'd had via Myspace and other social media sites was nothing compared to the national attention I received via Yahoo. In the old days, I'd just delete the occasional profanity-laced insult; during the Yahoo contest, I could only scroll, in quiet disbelief, through hundreds of comments describing the many ways in which I was worthless, a moron, and a whore. It was my first real taste of how dark things can get when you choose to live part of your life in the public eye.

But I also left the contest with a renewed sense of hope. For every jerk who said something gross online, I met some really positive and creative people. And the massive boost I'd received to my social media following seemed like a confirmation of what I had always thought to be true: That what I was doing wasn't crazy. That I just had to keep putting all the pieces together. That I had to have faith that, eventually, it would all lead somewhere.

So I said good-bye to the friends I had made in New York and boarded the plane back to Pennsylvania, believing in my gut that I would somehow figure it all out. I had to.

ORBITING MACWORLD

AFTER PLACING SECOND IN THE *YAHOO! TALENT SHOW***, I HAD EVERY IN-TENTION OF CONTINUING MY DAILY ROUTINE; MY PLAN WHEN I GOT BACK TO PITTSBURGH WAS TO KEEP DOING EXACTLY WHAT I HAD BEEN DOING.** Dez and I continued to make ridiculous videos, including one called "Parkour," produced under the *Mommy Pack My Lunch* banner (and inspired, obviously, by my fellow *Yahoo! Talent Show* finalists, the *actually* talented group Renzhe Parkour). We headed to downtown Carnegie, the Pittsburgh suburb in which we lived, to film ourselves freerunning and speed vaulting and cat leaping on the street. The joke was that as we bragged, documentary-style, about how long we'd been practicing the art of parkour (at the top of the video I said I was twenty-two years old and had been doing parkour for twenty-five years), how incredibly hard we trained, and how *amazing* our skills were (Dez looked to the camera to explain that "Justine has been able to jump over buildings . . . yeah, *buildings*"; I described, with faux modesty, the time I "saved a baby's life"), the viewer could clearly see our "skills" for what they were: We barely managed to hop over small cracks in the sidewalk. I performed awkward, graceless pirouettes in

the street for no apparent reason. At one point, I wrapped my arms around a parking meter while Dez struggled to lift my legs in the air. At another, Dez tried (and failed) to leap over one of the decorative blue bollards lining Carnegie's picturesque Main Street.

What I hadn't planned on, however, were the aftereffects of all that *Yahoo! Talent Show* exposure. Over the course of the contest, some of my videos had been featured prominently on the Yahoo home page (which had an online readership in the tens of millions); meanwhile, press releases related to the contest results had been distributed to newspapers and media outlets across the country. That national exposure, as it turns out, led to some minor press coverage at home, and by the end of 2006 I was actually starting to get some job offers.

The first email came from Groovr, a new social networking platform that functioned a little like Myspace meets Foursquare: you could "check in" at different locations via your cell phone, as well as upload photos, videos, and text. Each time you changed location, an alert would be sent out to your Groovr contact list (providing an efficient way to stalk your friends in real time). I was hired to create several promotional videos for the site.

The second came from Alex Lindsay. True to his word, we had kept in touch following PodCamp Pittsburgh, but I never could have been prepared for *his* email.

At the time—late December 2006—we were mere weeks away from the start of Macworld, the annual Apple trade show in San Francisco. The event had been going on since the mid-1980s; by the mid- to late 1990s, however, following Jobs's return to Apple as interim CEO, it had started to resemble a rock concert more than a tech conference.

Thousands of people showed up each year to watch Jobs unveil the newest and most innovative Apple products: the updated Mac operating system, OS X, in 2000; iTunes (2001); the GarageBand app (in 2004, for which musician John Mayer made a surprise appearance onstage); the iPod Shuffle (2005). By the close of 2006, anticipation about what he might reveal next was at a fever pitch.

In addition to launching new Apple products, Macworld was the place for start-up companies, gadget makers, and Apple accessory vendors to show off their stuff. At Macworld, attendees could interact with brand-new products firsthand. Accordingly, Macworld was a huge draw for reporters, bloggers, and tech experts, who flocked to San Francisco in order to review the latest tech for their viewers and readers. Which is exactly why the folks from *MacBreak*—a popular podcast dedicated to all things Apple, produced by Leo Laporte's TWiT.tv and Alex Lindsay's Pixel Corps—would be attending.

In fact, that's why Alex was reaching out: The *MacBreak* crew was looking for a new host, someone who could roam around the Moscone Center to interview vendors and attendees on camera. He wanted to know, did *I* want to do it?

It had been my dream to go to Macworld for as long as I could remember. I'd be at the epicenter of all things Apple. I'd be *working* on behalf of *MacBreak*. Better yet, I'd be in the same place, at the same time, as my personal idol, Steve Jobs.

As far back as seventh grade, when my classmates were writing book reports on U.S. presidents or major-league athletes or actors and entertainers, I was writing about the CEO of Apple Computer. The response from my peers was usually in the ballpark of "What the hell . . . ?" or "Who's Steve Jobs?" but by then I'd read all about the history of Apple—as well as Jobs's triumphant return to the company he had founded—and I was obsessed.

As I got older and learned more about graphic design, photography, and animation, Apple's products only got sexier and sleeker. The candy-colored iMac G3 gave way to the MacBook's more sophisticated aluminum shell. The introduction of the first iPod brought with it those now-iconic bright white headphones. The choices Apple made with regard to their products both informed and impacted me as a designer. These days, my preference for simple, modern aesthetics is echoed in just about everything I do, including the way my apartment is decorated. People often ask why my home is wall-to-wall white and stark as an insane asylum; I have to tell them I'm going for the "Apple Store look."

By college, my love and respect for Apple and its founder was so well known among my friends that I was given a framed head shot of Steve Jobs for my birthday (incidentally, by a guy who was also named Steve). The photo earned a proud spot on my desk next to my computer; you can see it in a number of the videos I've made over the years. Probably a few *too* many.

It wasn't just the cool gadgets or the sleek product design or the brash and charismatic CEO, though; over the years, I had fallen in love with Apple's culture. I was a huge fan of Apple's "think different" campaign, the seeds of which had been planted at Macworld 1997, when Jobs said this:

> *I think you still have to think differently to buy an Apple computer. The people who buy them do think different. They are the creative spirits in this world, and they're out to change the world. . . . A lot of people think they're crazy, but in that craziness we see genius.*

That idea resonated with me. It meant something to me. It felt personal. So, did I want to go to Macworld?

Uh, *yeah*. I told Alex I'd be happy to do it.

. . .

A few days before my flight, I reached out to several of my online friends who lived on the West Coast, including Karen Nguyen, who'd be attending with the entire Jumpcut crew.

Shortly after arriving in San Francisco, I met with Alex at his Pixel Corps headquarters. I was introduced to the rest of the *MacBreak* team, including Leo Laporte, whom I recognized immediately from all those afternoons binge-watching *TechTV* with my grandmother. I still had my Palm Treo with the trusty stylus, and I hadn't so much as put it down since my arrival—it didn't take Leo very long to ask me what in the world I was doing with it.

"Oh, I'm tweeting," I said.

Leo looked at me quizzically. He hadn't heard of Twitter yet.

"It'll be cool one day. I promise," I said. And then I pressured him to sign up for an account, just like I'd pressured everyone else in my life, at some point, to sign up for something.

David Tate
@davidjtate

+ Follow

The_Leo and iJustine = The Laurel and Hardy of Twitter.

8:58 PM - 28 Jan 2007

I was still hanging out in the Pixel Corps offices when Steve Jobs was scheduled to begin his keynote speech. I didn't have a press pass to get in the actual room with him, so I watched via streaming video as he took the stage, wearing his customary black turtleneck and jeans, and said simply: "Thank you for coming. We're going to make some history together today."

He wasn't kidding. After talking for twenty minutes about the success of the iPod and Apple's growing share of the digital music market, after offering up some financial updates and progress reports, he was ready to unveil the biggest thing yet: the launch of the original iPhone.

I really can't overstate how exciting this was—rumors about Apple entering the mobile phone market had been swirling for years, but I think the actual end result beat out even the wildest expectations. Every time Jobs demonstrated a new, never-before-seen feature of the phone—visual voicemail; "pinch" technology; something called an accelerometer, which allowed for both portrait and landscape view—the crowd erupted in frenzied applause and whistles and cheering. My favorite part of the whole morning, however, came at the very beginning of the presentation, when he finally gave the audience a glimpse of the phone's ultra-slim profile and extra-large screen, taking care to point out the complete lack of a physical keyboard.

"Now, how are we going to communicate [without a keyboard]?" he asked, pacing back and forth across the stage. "We don't want to carry a mouse around, right? So, what are we going to do? Oh! A stylus! We're going to use a stylus!"

He paused for the briefest of moments, just long enough for people in the audience to raise an eyebrow—really, a stylus?—before continuing: "*No.* Who wants a stylus? You have to get them and put them away and you lose them. Blech. *Nobody* wants a stylus."

I remember looking down at my stupid Palm Treo—the same phone that inspired the "Have You Seen My Stylus?" video—with something like disgust. Suddenly, it was clunky and awkward and ugly in my hand. I didn't want a stylus anymore, either. Steve was right.

In total, Jobs spoke for about ninety minutes about the phone, its service provider, its price point, and its features. At any other tech conference, a ninety-minute speech about a cell phone would've been mind-numbing; at Macworld, it was fun. To demonstrate the phone's calling features, he made a prank call to Starbucks and ordered four thousand lattes. To go. To announce new partnerships with other major tech companies, he briefly invited to the stage the CEOs of Google, Cingular, and—in a weird sort of "it's a small world" moment—Yahoo. (Just two months earlier, I had watched a video of Jerry Yang announcing the first-ever *Yahoo! Talent Show,* in which I ended up placing second; now here we both were at Macworld in San Francisco. It was surreal.) All morning Jobs, with contagious enthusiasm, punctuated his speech with a simple, charming refrain: "Isn't that cool?"

And it was cool! By the time he finished his keynote, Apple stock was up 8.3 percent and everyone at Macworld was itching to get an up-close-and-personal look at the world's most revolutionary phone. At the time, however, there were only two of them even in existence: Jobs's personal model, and a display model set to rotate slowly on a turntable inside a tamper-proof glass tube for the duration of the conference. Since the actual iPhone wouldn't be available for purchase for another six months, people crowded around that display model, pushing their noses up to the glass and snapping pictures and video, like tourists gawking at the *Mona Lisa*.

Distracted as I was by the phone (obviously I took a video standing beside the display model, too), I was at Macworld because I had a job to do. The folks from *MacBreak* set me up with a mic and a camera guy, and I functioned a bit like a field reporter, roaming around the floor of the Moscone Center and interviewing vendors and attendees about the coolest gadgets and tech. Big in 2007: ETCHamac, a service that provided custom laser engraving on personal media devices, allowing you to have an original drawing or design etched right onto the surface of your MacBook or iPod; a product called IntelliScanner, which made it possible to digitally inventory the items in your home (e.g., DVDs, groceries, your wine collection) using existing bar codes; and—my personal favorite, as well as one of Macworld's Best of Show winners—the Modbook, an after-market modification that turns a MacBook into a state-of-the-art pen tablet.

Macworld was my first on-camera hosting job, and though I had plenty of experience making weird videos about microwavable oatmeal, interpretive dance, and launching fruit at the heads of my friends, it took me a minute or two to get the hang of it—you can hear my voice wavering ever so slightly during some of the interviews. I loved it, though; even when my job was done, I still spent the duration of Macworld running around meeting and talking to people.

Karen Nguyen and I, meanwhile, had become fast friends. She would later write on her blog that not only was I the first person she'd gotten to know online and later meet IRL but a unifying trait among all of her friends is that (1) they're "a bit weird" and (2) "very much okay with it." Which is probably why we got along so well, since that's pretty much how I felt about all of my friends, too.

It was Karen who appeared with me on *Nightline* and *Good Morning America,* after I told the roving reporter that I'd been an Apple user "since I came out of my mom." (It was sort of ironic that I was there functioning as a reporter, but I so catastrophically blew it when the reporter from ABC interviewed *me*.) I was also with Karen, wandering from booth to booth in the convention hall, when we spotted a guy wearing a webcam strapped to his baseball cap. That guy, it turns out, was Justin Kan.

Justin, a twenty-three-year-old entrepreneur and Yale graduate, explained that he was live-streaming; that is, broadcasting footage from the camera to the Internet, which viewers could watch in real time. Though streaming technology wasn't exactly new—the popular website JenniCam, for example, which followed the dorm room exploits of then college student Jennifer Ringley, launched in the mid-1990s; streaming pornography sites have also existed for at least that long—it was Justin and the fellow cofounders of his company who took the technology mobile: they rigged a backpack to carry a laptop (to support their proprietary streaming software), two cellular-data wireless Internet cards (including a backup to prevent the stream from crashing), and an extra battery. It was small, compact, and easy to use. It was also pretty amazing—Justin's company made it possible for anyone to broadcast live from anywhere. In fact, the company's original objective was to produce and sell the backpacks on a large scale for just that purpose. (The focus of his company would eventually shift, but not before Justin himself was credited with popularizing the term *lifecasting*.)

Justin and I hit it off immediately—the similarity even of our names did not go unnoticed—and I asked him to keep me posted on his company's evolution and progress. In the days and weeks imme-diately following Macworld, he would become just another friend I'd made based on our similar interests; with time, however, his friend-ship would represent another strange example of how someone I met completely at random would wind up having a major effect on the en-tire course of my life. I got to thinking about that while on the floor of the Moscone Center, in fact, about how all things, even the seemingly bad ones, seem to happen for a reason. If I'd never taken the horrible job with the chiropractor, for example, I might not have uploaded so many videos to the web out of sheer boredom. Had I not uploaded so many videos, I may never have entered the *Yahoo! Talent Show* or gone to PodCamp. And had I never gone to PodCamp, I almost certainly wouldn't have ended up at Macworld in San Francisco. I remember looking around and feeling grateful: I had made it to the West Coast, to the seat of American technology. And by the time it was all over, I knew I wanted to move there.

ONE NIGHT ONLY

NEARLY FIFTY THOUSAND PEOPLE SHOWED UP AT MACWORLD IN 2007.
It was record-setting attendance, a 19 percent jump over the previous
year, and being on the floor of the Moscone Center gave me an appreciation for the massive size and scale of the tech world—from the enormous quantity of companies that were innovating new gadgets and
games to the thousands and thousands of people who, like me, identi-
fied as "geeks," and who were just as excited to be at the convention as
I was. By late January 2007, however, I was getting a sense for just how
small the tech world can be, too. In fact, if I had been playing Six Degrees of Separation with people in the tech community, it felt as though
I had dropped, overnight, from six degrees to just one or two. Leo and
Alex had given me some incredible access and exposure, and following
my debut as a host on *MacBreak,* I was gaining some traction—some
minor blogs and press outlets started calling me a "rising star" in the
geek world. (Which sounds like a contradiction in terms, doesn't it?)

I made my first appearance on *net@night,* a popular call-in show
hosted by Leo and his colleague Amber MacArthur. The show was broadcast live via TalkShoe (the same company Dez and I used for *Mommy Pack
My Lunch*), and the recorded version was later distributed as a podcast

available for purchase in stores like iTunes. (In case you were wondering, we chatted mainly about Twitter, Groovr, and Steve Jobs.) Around the same time, I was asked to come on *Geek Riot,* a Pittsburgh-based podcast created and hosted by Shawn Smith. By sheer coincidence, *Geek Riot* (which by all accounts had a pretty small listening base) ended up with a time slot on TalkShoe immediately following *net@night*—this was a bit like finding out *The Simpsons* is going to be your show's lead-in; Shawn's audience began to grow exponentially. I appeared for the first time on his weekly Sunday-night broadcast in late January; by the following week, Shawn had brought me on as an official cohost.

Before long I received a call from the folks at xTrain, an online learning website that offered classes in the digital arts (graphic and web design, photography, etc.). They wanted to hire me to host something called *60 Second Guru,* which was pretty much what it sounds like—a sixty-second tutorial hosted by an "expert" in the field—so they flew me to Dallas, where the company is headquartered. I was happy to discover that xTrain is partnered with Splash Media, one of the most technologically advanced television studios in the world. Let me tell you, the place is amazing—all the cameras are completely computer guided from the control room; the studio itself is basically one giant blue screen.

I ended up shooting several episodes of *60 Second Guru,* including one called "How to Create Viral Videos" (which is sort of ironic, since I had never technically made one before). Instead of the serious, straightforward manner in which the spots were usually filmed, however, I used all that state-of-the-art equipment to make some more absurdist, tongue-in-cheek comedy. At the top of the video, I vaulted over the anchor's desk. Then I proceeded to have a strange, nonsensical conversation with Chris, the show's technical director, about parkour. I explained what the word *viral* meant (because back then most people didn't actually know, if you can believe it), and then I suggested that capturing a "happy accident" on film would likely lead to viral success—cue shots of me tripping and falling all over Dallas, just like I'd done in the aisles of Walmart back in Pittsburgh. I couldn't tell you why, but the folks at xTrain must have been pleased with the results, because I ended up returning to Dallas three or four times that year.

Not long after my trip to Dallas, I headed to Los Angeles to meet with the team behind Groovr. It was perhaps the most bizarre introduction to L.A. possible—we ended up at a string of nightclubs and private parties, including one where Stephen Baldwin asked me for a stick of gum, and another at billionaire Paul Allen's house. (As in the cofounder of Microsoft, Paul Allen.) For some reason, Axl Rose was performing there. I remember looking around and thinking, *What the hell? Is this what L.A. is really like?* (As I would learn years later, however, that is not what L.A. is really like. At least, that's not what L.A. is like for *me*. I prefer spending my free time at home, in my sweatpants, playing video games.)

Justine Ezarik
@ijustine

🔲 Follow

I explained the internet to axl rose lastnight. I love that being a dork is accepted..... Or at least in my mind, anyways.

11:33 AM - 25 Feb 2007

None of these jobs, by the way, were resulting in huge paydays—in fact, all of the companies I was working for were start-ups. Whereas in the old days, I'd been "hired" as a photographer by local bands in Pittsburgh (and paid in CDs and concert tickets), now I was being hired by companies that didn't have a lot of cash flow and being paid, essentially, in plane tickets and travel accommodations. As the amount of traveling I was doing increased, I'd basically try to leapfrog my way across the country by patchworking flights together—Groovr might cover a Pacific-bound flight, while xTrain might get me to Dallas and back home again. I was more than happy to work with the companies to make all this happen, but I was broke.

I had a chance to change that when another start-up—a blog about emerging tech, this one with a lot of money behind it—suddenly offered me a full-time job. I flew to Philadelphia to meet with a member of the team; for some reason, the guy was obviously trying to impress me, because he showed up at the airport in a stretch limousine (which was both awkward and unnecessary). He also offered me a *huge* starting salary.

It would have been easy to cash in—it certainly would have alleviated most of my financial concerns, of which I had plenty—but I knew there was no way I could take the job (or any of the others I would be offered over the next few years). I had been through hell working for the chiropractor, and I was not going to go back to that; I was never going to sign up for another full-time job where I'd be stuck taking orders from someone else. Besides, most of the companies I met with during that time wanted exclusivity, anyway. (Meaning I wouldn't even be able to post content on my own website or YouTube channel, which was not something I was prepared to give up.) I was going to keep working for myself, broke or not.

In between various graphic design projects and consulting and hosting gigs, I continued creating my own original content and posting it online. I also refocused on *Mommy Pack My Lunch*, which had slowly morphed from a fake-news show into a kind of absurdist, two-woman sketch comedy troupe. When Dez and I scheduled a last-minute vacation to Florida, I got the idea to launch MPML TV. The plan was to broadcast (and by "broadcast," I mean post videos online; I don't think we ever actually attempted to live-stream) from various locations around the country.

Unfortunately, MPML TV lasted all of two episodes. In episode one I employed a hideously bad fake British accent and held up a pink snapper I had found on sale at a fish market. Episode two featured Dez and me taking turns holding a seven-foot yellow python named Merlin (for no reason other than that we saw Merlin's owner walking down the street while we were sitting at an outdoor restaurant, waiting for our food). I can't *imagine* why this show didn't become an immediate hit.

Back home in Pittsburgh, we returned to doing what we did "best": we filmed a more traditional *MPML* video, wherein we went tanning—in shorts and sunglasses—on a snowdrift. Despite the failure of MPML TV, I assumed we were doing *something* right: within a few days, "Tanning in the Snow" became a Revver Editor's Pick; separately, I was named a "featured content creator." At the same time, the clip of Dez throwing an apple at my head became a "featured video" on Yahoo. I also hit my ten thousandth Myspace friend.

Me: It's positively balmy *out here! Dez: I hate you for making me do this.*

Justine Ezarik 🐦
@ijustine
+⌄ Follow

who wants to be my 10,000 myspace friend?
http://www.myspace.com/ijustine

↩ ⇄ ★ •••
9:03 PM - 28 Jan 2007

Justine Ezarik 🐦
@ijustine
+⌄ Follow

10k friend contest over.. That was quick.

↩ ⇄ ★ •••
9:12 PM - 28 Jan 2007

• • •

While all of this was going on, Justin Kan had been busy with the official launch of his company. He called it Justin.tv, and the concept was simple: wearing the baseball cap fitted with his webcam—the same one he'd worn at Macworld—he would film himself twenty-four hours a day, seven days a week, and broadcast the content online. Viewers could interact with him, as well as with each other, in the Justin.tv chat room. Part of the draw was that, for Justin, nothing was off-limits: the camera followed him everywhere, on dates, to bed at night, even into the bathroom.

The amount of press coverage centered around the launch was pretty major: the *San Francisco Chronicle* ran a front-page story; Justin was interviewed on the *Today* show by Ann Curry. According to sources at the company, the website hit a million page views within just two weeks.

I had been watching, too, of course, not only because Justin was my new Internet friend but because Justin.tv was fascinating. Unlike some other early lifecasting sites, this wasn't a static camera positioned somewhere in Justin's room—viewers went wherever he went. It was near un-precedented, as well as addictive. In fact, the only downsides that I saw (at least, from a viewer's perspective) were that Justin didn't often interact with people in the chat room—since he was busy launching a start-up, a large portion of his day was spent sitting around, working. The camera was also positioned outward, documenting not so much Justin (as if he was the star of the show) but rather his point of view. (In the early days, Justin once appeared to fall asleep at his desk, so viewers were stuck looking at an awkwardly up-close shot of his arm for about an hour.)

By April things were going well enough that Justin needed to attend some private investor meetings (during which he obviously wouldn't be able to wear the camera). Rather than go off-line, how-ever, he wanted someone else to take over for the day. And that's when he reached out to me. He wanted to know, did I want to do it?

Of course I wanted to do it! On one condition: Dez had to come with me.

Revver ended up sponsoring my trip, in part because Justin's in-vestor meetings—and, accordingly, my debut on Justin.tv—happened to be taking place at the same time as the first-ever Web 2.0 Expo (they were virtually guaranteed to get some press out of it). So, I headed back to San Francisco and the Moscone Center. All of a sudden, I was right back where I had started.

What I hadn't expected was just how, uh, *festive* this trip would turn out to be. It was April 2007—more than five years after the dot-com crash of the early 2000s, but still several months shy of the first waves of the impending global recession—and tech start-ups, with major in-fusions of cash from venture capitalists, were booming. As a result, Web 2.0 Expo had turned into a giant party—and I mean that pretty much

Getting the hang of this live-streaming thing, with Dez and Karen.

literally; parties lined the streets of San Francisco's SoMa neighborhood. (That's short for "South of Market" Street, by the way; the SoMa district also happens to be home to CNET, Twitter, BitTorrent, Yelp, and a host of other tech company headquarters.) The night Dez and I arrived in town (the night before I would don the Justin.tv camera), we tagged along with Justin to a party for the Snap Shots launch, and then to a nightclub called 111 Minna for a Netvibes event. The place was packed. A line of people stretched down the block. The bar was open. *Wired* magazine would later call it "the hottest shindig on the Web 2.0 Expo calendar."

There was *a lot* going on that week. Dez and I landing in the middle of it all was another right-place-right-time kind of coincidence.

The next morning, I put on the hat and the backpack, and we were off. Dez and I headed to a local Starbucks and took a cable car to Union Square. I ran into a panhandler singing and dancing on the street. Since he was dressed in a spectacular purple suit—with a matching fedora—I decided to dance with him, naturally. Then we talked about George Benson for a while. He encouraged me to google him.

We swung by an Apple Store, where I told an employee that I was visually impaired, that the camera I was wearing was "hardwired to my brain" to help me see. (I think he bought it.) We had snacks with the co-founder of Hot or Not, James Hong. Since I didn't know the streets of San Francisco well, Karen, my Jumpcut friend, spent most of the day watching the feed and sending me directions via text message. After lunch we headed to the expo. That night we met up with Justin and his friends for dinner.

The experience, all in all, was fun. I wasn't particularly concerned with the viewers' reaction—there just wasn't much pressure to be funny or entertaining since it was only a one-day commitment. In fact, I barely paid any mind to the chat room. The only time I really pulled the laptop out of the backpack was to occasionally confirm that our battery hadn't died on us or that the stream wasn't down.

But it must have gone well, because a few weeks later, Justin called back. He asked if I wanted to try it again. Only this time, he wanted to know: Did I want to take over indefinitely?

iJUSTINE.TV

I MAYBE SHOULD HAVE PAID MORE ATTENTION TO THE FACT THAT LIFECASTING, AT LEAST FOR JUSTIN, DIDN'T COME WITHOUT COMPLICATIONS. Within two weeks of launching his site, he'd already gone through four different phone numbers in an attempt to halt the avalanche of prank calls he was suddenly getting at all hours of the day and night. One afternoon, a delivery guy showed up at his door with sixty-three dollars' worth of pizza. Though perhaps a *happy* side effect, Justin started fielding a lot of random requests for blind dates—he even went on a few, and was sometimes stood up on camera. But the most dramatic Internet prank happened just three or four days after going live: Justin was typing away at his laptop one night, hip-hop music blaring, when a handful of San Francisco Police Department officers burst into his apartment, guns drawn. "Did somebody get stabbed in the chest here?" one of them shouted.

I was watching Justin.tv when it happened—I held my breath as Justin, still wearing the camera on his head, threw his hands up into the air. I watched in disbelief as the officers cased his apartment, shining flashlights in corners of rooms, brusquely questioning Justin and his friends. I listened as he tried to explain his "job" to the cops—"Uh, tech company," he said, obviously still startled—as well as the reason someone might have called in such an outrageous allegation: "Uh, it's probably someone . . . spoofing our phone number . . . as a prank," he said. It was scary and it was serious; you got the immediate, unmistakable sense that when it came to the Internet, anything could—and probably *would*—happen. (If you weren't watching Justin.tv in those days, by the way, you can still see the whole thing on YouTube.)

Still, when Justin explained that he was ready to begin expanding his site—the fact that our names were so similar perhaps made me a shoo-in to host the second Justin.tv channel—I couldn't help but feel excited. From the first silly videos I'd posted online to the madness of competing in the *Yahoo! Talent Show* to attending Macworld, I'd seen some of the possibilities and opportunities available on the Internet. Even though I was aware of the effect it already had on Justin's life, live-streaming seemed like an almost appropriate next step. I didn't put much thought into what the potential consequences of broadcasting every minute of my life would be; I wasn't worried about any kind of fallout or blowback. In fact, I actually believed, though it's ridiculous thinking about it now, that live-streaming my life would be *easier*—instead of filming and editing and uploading videos, I'd just turn a camera on and be done.

Oh, how incredibly naive I was. What an idiot.

The folks from Justin.tv sent me a box of equipment: a laptop with an extra battery, a webcam, a ball cap (which I would eventually replace with something, well, cuter), and an integrated Sprint EVDO card. We set the date for the premiere of my new channel as May 29, 2007. And then there was only one thing left to do before going live: tell my friends.

I called Anthony (whom I had met years earlier through Steve, the guy who'd given me the framed picture of Steve Jobs for my birthday) and asked if he wanted to hang out. We had had a casual friendship for years, but we'd grown considerably closer in the previous month or two, not long after he started working in the casting office for a Spike TV miniseries called *The Kill Point*. Anthony had put out a call to his friends, looking for extras to fill out a bank robbery scene in Market Square (in downtown Pittsburgh), and Dez and I immediately volunteered, largely because the show starred John Leguizamo and I have been obsessed with him since 1993, when he played Luigi in the *Super Mario Bros.* movie. The shoot was six long days and there was a *ton* of downtime—there always is on major film and television sets—which gave Anthony and me just long enough to discover that we had a naturally antagonistic, brother-sister kind of relationship (read: we made fun of each other a lot). He was hilarious and silly and usually up for anything. When I sat down to tell him about my plans, though, I couldn't help feeling a little nervous.

"So, do you remember when I went to San Francisco and did the one-day experiment with Justin.tv?" I asked him. "I wore the camera on my head and streamed the entire thing to the Internet?"

"Yeah . . . ?" he said.

"Well . . . they want me to do it again. Indefinitely."

Anthony lifted his eyebrows and thought for a moment. "So, what you're telling me is," he said after a beat, "the next time we hang out, the Internet will be watching?"

"Yeah."

He laughed. "Okay," he said, smiling. And this is why I love Anthony—he was totally on board (although he did tell me he thought I was crazy).

I told CJ, too—you remember him, the one who wanted to be a cop when we were kids?—and his reaction was something along the lines of "Wait. You're doing *what*?" It turned out to be a common response. Most people I spoke with were surprised and/or confused, if not rendered entirely speechless. Virtually everyone, however, was supportive. Not one single person said that I shouldn't do it, or even intimated that it might be a bad idea.

Except, maybe, for Dez, who was skeptical from the very beginning. And really, who could blame her? After all, we weren't just friends and coworkers—we lived together. Whether she liked it or not, being my best friend and roommate would mean a significant amount of time on camera for her, too. Virtually nothing between us would be private. Everything would be broadcast online.

In a lot of ways, I had kind of dragged Dez kicking and screaming into my crazy Internet world. She'd been game for almost all of it—we'd had tons of fun making silly videos, and *MPML* was something we were pursuing not just for fun but as a kind of *job*—but she wasn't quite as enthusiastic as me. She wasn't obsessed with tech and computers like I was. In fact, I'm pretty sure she was often horrified by the effect that emerging tech had on my life. She resisted signing up for Twitter, for example, largely because she saw firsthand that my phone beeped and buzzed and chimed and rang all day long. She had no interest in that.

I think she was also more affected by Internet "haters" than I was. Months earlier, we had received an email to our Myspace account from someone at another comedy site. It was weird: he'd been following us since the *Yahoo! Talent Show,* but then one day, out of the blue, he just decided to email us to explain all the reasons why we weren't funny and to implore us to just "give up." She was able to keep a sense of humor about it, but for Dez, I don't think the positives ever outweighed the negatives. She was all about graphic design, photography, local Pittsburgh indie bands, the stuff we had originally bonded over—she hadn't signed up for any of this. She was (and is!) such a good friend, however, that she went along with the live-stream anyway, for no reason other than that it was important to me. Have I told you yet how amazing Desirée is? Seriously. I am *so* lucky to have her in my life.

As the launch date grew closer, I started to set some ground rules for myself. For one thing, I certainly wasn't going to be taking the camera into the bathroom. Ever. I wasn't dating anyone at the time, so I knew *that* wouldn't be a problem, either. (In fact, I had recently broken up with someone who used to get insanely jealous about the random Myspace comments I sometimes received from strangers, which is especially ironic seeing as how we broke up because I accidentally came across a chat from his ex that read, in part, "Thanks for last night.") Security was also a major concern. I knew I would take pains to hide my actual location from the Internet, in particular my and Dez's address. I'd come a long way from filming the Ninja Turtles video in my backyard—I realized I'd have to hide the camera in my purse whenever I left the house, in order to obscure my apartment and the streets immediately surrounding it. After seeing what had happened to Justin, I didn't want anyone to know where we lived.

The night before the camera was scheduled to go on, Dez and I went out to celebrate (mourn?) our last night of freedom. We went to dinner at Chili's and then to a concert to see a mutual friend's band play. I ended up meeting a guy there named Cory, who had seen me filming this crazy woman dancing like a loon in the middle of the bar. After saying hello (to Cory, not the crazy woman), I quickly steered the conversation to Apple computers (classic Justine). As we continued chatting, I figured I might as well tell him about the project, too.

"So starting tomorrow, I'm going to be live-streaming my entire life on the web. Every day. All the time," I told him.

"Wait. You're doing *what*?" he said.

I wasn't kidding when I said that virtually everyone I told had that exact same response.

At that moment, however, I realized the only people I *had* told about Justin.tv were my friends; they more or less expected this kind of thing from me. Hearing the shock from a total stranger gave me a twinge of anxiety. Maybe putting almost every detail of my life on the web *wasn't* such a great idea?

Here's another funny thing about the Internet, though: Cory ended up casually watching the live-stream and we kept in touch (off camera, usually via email and text message), even though it would be roughly seven years before I'd see him in person again. We're still friends to this day. In fact, he's one of the people who encouraged me to write a book! (Thanks, Cory!) And it's all thanks to live-streaming!

Anyway, I didn't have all that much time to feel weird about my decision, because the next morning I went live. Justine.tv was officially on.

I fell into a kind of routine fairly quickly: I'd wake up and greet the chat room, say hello, ask how everyone was doing. Then I'd pop into the shower (obviously, I didn't film that, either) and start the twenty-minute drive to Crazy Mocha, where I preferred to do the bulk of my work. Because that's the other thing: I wasn't getting paid to live-stream. Justin.tv, after all, was just another in a long line of start-ups—in fact, those guys were spending tens of thousands of dollars a month, essentially all of their seed funding, just to cover their Internet costs. Meanwhile, I was still trying to make ends meet by way of free-lance graphic design work, video editing, and the occasional hosting gig. So every day, I'd arrive at Crazy Mocha and start unloading my "office." Let me give you an idea of what this insanity looked like:

1. MacBook Pro 1.16 Intel Core Duo (my personal laptop, the one I did actual editing work on)
2. Apple Mighty Mouse
3. Treo 700p
4. iPhone 8G
5. Incase Fitted Sleeve for iPhone
6. Logitech QuickCam Fusion (mounted to the bill of my hat)
7. Western Digital 1TB My Book external hard drive
8. Crazy Mocha beverage
9. Sony VAIO VGN-TVN15P (the laptop I'd received from Justin.tv, which I used mostly for streaming purposes)

Not pictured:

10. Canon SD800 (for still photography)
11. Panasonic PV-GS300 3.1MP 3CCD MiniDV (for video)
12. Integrated Sprint EVDO card

It sort of looked as though I were operating a portable NORAD command station from that tiny Formica tabletop, doesn't it? Some days, I'd eat breakfast, lunch, and dinner there—not to mention drink a whole lot of coffee—before eventually packing up and heading home.

On days when I needed to be a bit more mobile, I'd just wear the camera on my hat and carry the VAIO around in my purse (the laptop was configured not to go into sleep mode when the lid was closed).

A peek at the Justin.tv chat rooms—I was live-streaming from Crazy Mocha.

Now for a couple of unexpected consequences of live-streaming, right off the bat: I slept with music on in those days (usually the gentle, soothing melodies of the nineties alt-rock band Tool, if you're wondering). Apparently, however, sleeping with music on is deceptive, because some of the viewers were so convinced that something was wrong with me that they started calling my parents' (then-listed) phone number.

"Is Justine dead?!" they'd ask. "We think she's dead."

My mother would have to explain that her daughter wasn't dead, she was just sleeping late.

Courtesy of Scott Beale

You would think this sort of thing would have been terrifying, that it would have completely freaked my poor parents out, but that's where the second unintended consequence of live-streaming comes in: it turns out that broadcasting yourself twenty-four hours a day gives a parent unfettered access to what his or her child is doing. (Who knew?) Since I was only twenty-three and hadn't been out on my own for that long, my parents were still pretty protective. In fact, they didn't just watch my Justin.tv channel, they *patrolled* it—it was on twenty-four hours a day in their house. Occasionally, the results were comical: like the time my mom called and told me not to buy the bathing suit I had just tried on—the one I was still holding in my hands—because my sister already owned the exact same one. Other times, though? Not so much. Like the time I was in Atlanta, drinking in a bar, and my mother called to yell at me for being out so late. "You don't know those people!" she said. "And you're drinking! You shouldn't be doing that!"

Eventually, if I was planning on being out late and/or drinking, my backup battery would conveniently "die" and the stream would shut down, affording me some much-needed privacy. Whoops. Sorry, Mom.

• • •

Despite the fact that live-streaming was a nonpaying enterprise (and I was still struggling to pay my bills), it didn't take long before I started feeling the pressure to *entertain*. I tried interacting with the chat room whenever possible. If I had a freelance job I was working on, for example, I might ask the viewers for feedback: What *do you think* of this video? Or, *how does* this logo look? Some mornings, I'd poll the chat room, asking for opinions about how I should spend the day. Other times, I'd convince Dez to walk the aisles of Walmart with me, just to have a reason to get out of the house. If all else failed, I'd just sit at my desk and field questions and requests (ranging from "How many gigs is your iPod?" to "I dare you to do the Chicken Dance" to "Take your shirt off") for hours.

For the most part, at least in the first few weeks of live-streaming, the viewers were supportive and cordial. There were absolutely gross and inappropriate and lewd comments, too—I mean, this was the Internet—but I was generally able to ignore them. Besides, I'd had some exposure to nastiness already. The worst things in the world had been said about me during the *Yahoo! Talent Show*. I figured, after that, live-streaming would be a walk in the park. I thought I had developed a thicker skin.

What I hadn't planned on were awful, unkind comments about my friends and family, including—maybe especially—about Dez, just by virtue of the fact that she was on camera so much. It was one thing for Internet trolls to attack me—I'd signed up for this. Insulting the people closest to me, though, was a whole other thing, for which I felt both awful and responsible.

I did have some help policing the chat room: over on Justin's channel, some particularly loyal viewers were granted moderator status, allowing them to completely block particularly abusive or rude viewers. Some of those moderators migrated over to my channel, and I also had the ability to grant moderator status to other viewers as I saw fit. And usually there were enough kind souls out there to ensure that someone was there to stick up for and defend me round-the-clock. Over time the moderators even started to organize themselves into shifts—for no money, compensation, or recognition other than having achieved moderator status, just because they wanted to be there, to ensure things were running relatively smoothly.

Even with the moderators, though, live-streaming would slowly begin to take its toll, not just on me, but on everyone around me. The question was: How long would I be able to hold out?

• • •

I had been live-streaming for only a few days—a week, maybe—when a company called Technology Evangelist offered to fly me to the Mall of America to document the release of the original iPhone. It was June, six long months since Macworld, and I'd been dying to get one. Unfortunately, I had two hundred dollars in my checking account. I had no credit cards. There was no way I could afford one. So I agreed to cover the launch, even though I knew I wouldn't be purchasing a phone for myself.

This was not something I was particularly ready or willing to admit to on camera, by the way. In the world of product reviews, it's common practice for companies to send out trial versions of their gadgets or software to editors and bloggers so they actually have something to write about—it's hard to recommend or evaluate a product, after all, if you've never so much as held it in your hand, let alone used it for a while. But I didn't have those kinds of connections. Even though I'd become an occasional host and spokesperson, even though I had a huge following on Myspace and I'd hit the five-thousand-friend limit on Facebook, there weren't yet a lot of viable options when it came to monetizing an Internet following. Making a career out of living your life online was still just too new a concept. I had to have faith that, eventually, this whole live-streaming thing would start to pay for itself.

But until then, I would head to Minnesota, courtesy of Technology Evangelist, where the iPhone was scheduled to go on sale at 6 p.m. I showed up relatively early in the morning and promptly got kicked out of the Apple Store (which was quickly becoming something of a habit; I'd been politely asked to leave Apple Stores in Pennsylvania, Texas, Georgia, New York, California, and now Minnesota, usually for unauthorized "video blogging," this time because they were banning all "media" until the launch). By 1:30 p.m. I had decided to interview the first person waiting in line, which turned out to be a young guy named Joe Dowdell. I did what I had, by then, grown accustomed to: I immediately asked if he was on Twitter (he was not), and then I dutifully explained all the reasons why Twitter was amazing and why he should join (until he did). Then I harassed the Internet to be Joe's friend, which seemed only fair. By three I'd been yelled at for juggling in the mall (now that I think about it, security was really tight at this thing). And by six, after spending roughly eight hours standing in a line for something I couldn't even purchase, Joe was welcomed into the store.

Justine Ezarik 🐦
@ijustine   👤 Follow

Everyone… @joe28753 is the first guy in line here at the MOA Apple store and I forced him to sign up for twitter. Be his friend :)

↩ ↺ ★ …
1:48 PM - 29 Jun 2007

I don't know who was more excited about the whole thing, though: Joe or me. Because he graciously agreed to perform his ceremonial "unboxing" not once but twice, so that I could film it for my live-stream and the guys from Technology Evangelist could capture the moment in HD video, but I just stood around screaming, "Oh my God, it's so beautiful!" like an idiot. Then I announced—without even asking Joe for *his* opinion—that this was "the best day of his life."

It was another one of those strange sort of coincidences: I mean, Joe could have been a huge jerk; he could have been way too tired to participate in my silliness (since he'd been camping outside the Apple Store all day); he could have politely asked the strange girl with the camera on

Celebrating the iPhone launch with Joe at the Mall of America, June 29, 2007.

her head to get the hell away from him. Instead, he was willing to let us share in his fun. I'm still Internet friends with Joe to this day, and I still think about him every time I attend a new iPhone launch—and it's all because he just happened to be the first in line for the original iPhone, and I just happened to be there to document it.

I flew back home to Pittsburgh, deliriously happy, only to find another surprise waiting: the people at Technology Evangelist had taken pity on me. They had bought me my very own iPhone.

• • •

So, I was kind of starting to get the hang of this live-streaming thing. In fact, sometimes I even found it *helpful*. In the period immediately following the release of the iPhone, I was rarely home for more than a few days at a time—I was traveling nonstop, to Los Angeles and San Francisco (usually for Justin.tv-related press, though sometimes to meet up with other tech companies, including the folks from Revver); down to Texas to shoot with xTrain; to Atlanta for something called the HOW Design Conference (also with xTrain); to New York to check out the Live Earth concert—and every time I hit the road, the chat room ended up being of unexpected assistance. For example, when I was sitting at the airport waiting for my flight to Minnesota, I didn't realize I was at the wrong gate until members of the chat room alerted me. (Because I am a forgetful person, I also asked for help locating my car in the parking garage when I got back to Pittsburgh.) On the drive to New York, I kept trying to use Google Maps, but the technology wasn't what it is today (that's a nice way of saying it pretty much sucked), so I utilized directions from my Internet friends. I still rely on the Internet—and I don't mean websites or social media platforms, but the actual people—to this day. Whenever I'm headed out of town, I ask for recommendations on things to do and see—it's like running a real-time web search, only better. It's crowdsourced.

Of course, there were a number of ways in which live-streaming was also starting to make life difficult, to put it mildly. For one thing, I was lugging around a ridiculous amount of equipment—extension cords and a power strip, in addition to my usual haul. TSA agents were actually starting to recognize me as I unpacked my carry-on bags at the security line. And then there was the time things got really scary.

I was headed back home from New York. I boarded the plane without incident, turning off my streaming equipment before take-off. The flight was uneventful, until we landed. Just as the cabin door opened, one of the flight attendants got on the loudspeaker: "Is there a Justine Ezarik here?" she asked.

I slowly raised my hand. "Um, yes?"

"Will you please stand up?" she said. "We're going to escort you off the plane now."

A sky marshal appeared out of nowhere, and I was immediately sick to my stomach. I couldn't figure out what I had done, but I knew it was bad—and it had to be something related to the live-stream. For all I knew, it was illegal to film at an airport. As I was being walked down the Jetway, into the terminal, it occurred to me that I was going to be led into some kind of private interrogation room. I didn't know what would happen when they got me in there so I started emphatically insisting that I needed to go to the bathroom.

I was halfway in the ladies' before I was booting up my laptop with one hand and trying to find Justin Kan's contact info in my new iPhone with the other. He answered on the second ring.

"Listen," I said frantically, "I didn't do anything, but I need you to wipe whatever I might have filmed at the airport from the Justin.tv servers."

"What?" he said.

"Just delete it!!" I screamed at him. "I don't care what you have to do, get rid of it. I think I'm in trouble." Meanwhile, I was busy trying to wipe any evidence off my computer's hard drive. (Which is stupid, of course, because any information I "deleted" could easily have been recovered.)

I threw my computer back together, splashed some water on my face, and came back out to face my interrogators. We continued to the dreaded little room, and a couple of airport employees started pummeling me with questions: *Who are you? What were you filming? Who were you talking to? What were you doing?* Obviously, someone must have seen me back in New York and thought talking to my computer and filming the airport seemed suspicious.

At first I tried to avoid saying anything about Justin.tv, but I realized that if they so much as googled me, they'd only wonder why I was lying. So, I began carefully trying to explain: "Well, I do this live-stream stuff? I make videos and put them online?"

This only seemed to confuse them further. "Well, who's watching it?" one of them asked.

"Um, people?" I said. "On the Internet?"

I was not helping myself.

After another hour or so of questioning—mostly along the lines of *Why would anyone want to watch a stranger on the Internet all day long?*—they finally let me go.

Looking back, I now know that security would have been heightened as a result of the 2007 London terror bombings—which could have been the cause for the suspicion relative to what I was doing. However, I have a blond-haired, blue-eyed friend who lives in Iceland; she got stopped so often at airport security that she finally freaked out one day and asked what was going on. A polite TSA representative explained, in a very matter-of-fact tone, that she fit their profile of an international drug smuggler. She dyed her hair brown the next day, and hasn't been stopped at airport security since. So, maybe that's what was going on? All I know for sure is that no one has ever questioned me again, and I film in airports all the time. I think about that day every time I whip my camera out, though—I'm telling you, it was so scary, I didn't even tweet about it.

• • •

Back home in Pittsburgh, I was either at the coffee shop or, increasingly, finding weird and interesting things to do on the live-stream. Some of my friends, meanwhile—in particular CJ and Anthony—had grown more and more interested in "helping," though probably to unexpected results. CJ, for example, got a little overexcited and revealed his private phone number online. Like, just to see what would happen. Years later he would tell me he was still getting random, middle-of-the-night phone calls from people.

Anthony, however, took a more creative, you might even say *artistic,* tack: he approached his debut on Justin.tv almost like an acting job. I think he fancied himself a kind of Jim Halpert to my Michael Scott—he thought he'd flash an exasperated look or two to the camera, in the faux-documentary style of *The Office,* and win over the audience.

It did not work out like that. The chat room immediately started tearing him down as soon as he made it on-screen. I've blocked most of this out, by the way, so I asked Anthony to jog my memory with regard to the details.

> *ANTHONY: Oh, I remember. As soon as I got to your apartment and waved to the camera, the insults started:*
>> *"Nice haircut."*
>> *"He doesn't dress very well."*
>> *"Why does he chew gum so hard?"*
>> *"She's too hot for him."*
> *Just warm, encouraging stuff right there. It didn't matter that we had made it abundantly clear that we weren't dating,*

that we were hanging out solely as friends. According to the chat room, I didn't deserve to be there. I was immediately cast as the villain, the guy who got to hang out with the hot girl while the Justin.tv viewers watched in silent rage.

Ugh, see what I mean? The funny thing about Anthony, though, is that not only was he not bothered by this, he was *into* it—especially when he saw the potential for interaction with the audience, especially when he began to understand what some of the viewers were really like.

One night we went to dinner at a local LongHorn Steakhouse. As per usual, I placed my hat with the mounted webcam on top of a napkin holder in order to get a wide shot of the table. Within twenty minutes, the phone calls started.

Every so often, our poor, confused-looking hostess would walk up to the table to tell me I had a phone call. I'd (reluctantly) walk up to the front, knowing full well the person on the other end of the line would be someone from the Internet, and then return to our table to confirm this to Anthony. "It's one of *them*," I said.

Prank phone calls, however, were clearly not exciting enough. Not long after we finished our meals, a chorus of voices singing "Happy Birthday" began echoing through the restaurant. Anthony and I were presented with a large hot-fudge sundae while the entire waitstaff of LongHorn Steakhouse serenaded me.

ANTHONY: So there we were, with a free dessert and a chat room full of viewers waiting for a reaction. I realized the incredible opportunity to have some fun, of course, so I turned to

125

*the camera, pulled the sundae right up to my face, and said,
"Thanks for the dessert, guys." Then I smugly took a giant bite.
The outrage was palpable.*

Obviously, Anthony liked antagonizing the trolls. And since we
had such a bicker-back-and-forth kind of relationship, it came naturally. We started acting out what were, essentially, elaborate skits on
camera. We'd go to restaurants and stage wild, over-the-top argu-
ments—we'd march away from the table as if in the middle of a huge
lovers' spat. I'd wiggle the webcam around, dramatically blurring the
image, while screaming and running through the parking lot. Here's
an example:

> ANTHONY
> (following Justine out of
> the restaurant, stomping
> his feet)
> Oh, that's right. Walk away. Just
> walk away . . .

> JUSTINE
> Don't even talk to me!

> ANTHONY
> (walking into a busy
> parking lot)
> Oh, look! We're in traffic . . .
> where *you* should play.

Justine stomps around the parking lot, yelling
and carrying on, refusing to get in Anthony's
car. Anthony drives slowly behind her, pleading

with her to get in. Finally, Justine gets in
the car. A door *SLAMS*.

> ANTHONY
> (disgusted)
> Typical shit.

> JUSTINE
> Don't say "shit" on my camera.

> ANTHONY
> . . . shit on your camera?

> JUSTINE
> Don't say "shit" on my camera!!

> ANTHONY
> (resigned)
> I should have just run you over.

Driving home after another explosive (completely staged) "fight." Poor Anthony,
people on the Internet still refer to him as "the worst date ever."

. . .

As the weeks and months flew by, I began making fewer and fewer edited videos to upload to the web, largely because my life in general was beginning to resemble one long, zany YouTube clip—all of my creative energy was going toward lifecasting. I was constantly racking my brain for silly (and hopefully entertaining) things to do for the sake of the broadcast. After purchasing a Steelcase Think Chair for my "office," for example, I decided to camp out in the massive cardboard box the chair had been shipped in; for two consecutive nights, I provided updates on how things were going "inside the box."

As the size of my audience continued to grow and the concept of live-streaming started to gain traction (by then Justin had launched several new channels on Justin.tv; there were at least four of us streaming round-the-clock now, including the Naked Cowboy, a Times Square street musician famous for walking around New York City in nothing but a cowboy hat, boots, and a pair of tighty-whities), I decided it was time to branch out. I started broadcasting to Ustream, as well as working with Viddler, an interactive video platform with inline tagging and commenting capability (meaning the comments were embedded right into the video feed itself). Viddler's (remarkably prescient) tagline at the time was "Brand Yourself." Basically, the site allowed you to customize the look of its video player, both by selecting the color (ostensibly to match your existing website's aesthetic) and to upload a personal logo, two features I took advantage of immediately. The result was that my content was *everywhere,* from well-established social networking platforms like Myspace to streaming platforms like

Justin.tv and Ustream to emerging sites in the video-sharing space, including Revver, Viddler, and YouTube.

It was in the middle of all this—early August 2007—that I received that unexpected package in the mail from AT&T. I unboxed what would soon become the infamous three-hundred-page phone bill while live-streaming, but as I flipped through each of the pages, I knew I'd make a separate, edited video about the experience, too. How could I not? It was the first time in months that I didn't have to invent a creative concept for an online clip; the entire premise—to juxtapose the massive success of the iPhone launch with the massive failure of AT&T's billing program—had practically fallen into my lap.

Still, the scale of the press attention the video received took my breath away. I had already been making videos on the Internet for five years; I'd been blogging for nearly a decade; I'd started attending every tech trade show in the country, but nothing I had ever done even came close to garnering this kind of traffic. Of course, none of the reporters from the major networks or the national newspapers knew who I was—to them I was just a girl with a text message addiction who'd received an unusually large phone bill. The mounting media coverage, however, drove traffic to my live-stream channels; meanwhile, my online presence helped to boost the visibility of the news articles, until the whole thing became one huge self-fulfilling circle. I hit 3 million views within ten days. It was madness. It was exhilarating. And all I could think was, well, *what in the world am I supposed to do now?*

One week later, AT&T announced—via a network-wide text message—that they would simplify their billing policies, removing itemized detail as the default option. I made a follow-up video, which received a fair amount of views at the time, although nothing even close to the original.

It's pretty natural to want to re-create viral success once you've experienced it; what I knew intuitively, however (and what the follow-up video perhaps confirms), is that you can't—there is no such thing as a viral video formula or guaranteed success on the Internet. The best you can do is to continue creating consistent content, continue connecting with people who like the same things you like, and use the momentum to carry you forward. Sustained success online isn't about going *viral*; it's about building a loyal community that knows what to expect (whether that's hard-hitting political commentary, video game playthroughs, or funny videos about nothing at all) when they visit your site.

The "300-page iPhone bill" brought with it a whole new level of interest in (and scrutiny of) the content I'd been posting online. One person who wasn't happy with the increased attention, though, was Dez. Neither one of us had been prepared for how intense the experience of live-streaming would be; neither one of us had any idea of the many ways it would slowly begin to alter our friendship. And whether we'd been willing to admit it or not, things had changed.

We had spent virtually every single day of the past five years together, but we suddenly weren't hanging out very much—in part because I was constantly headed out of town, but also because Dez had begun actively avoiding the camera. She'd even started spending nights away from the apartment, staying with friends, just to give herself a bit of a break. She didn't feel as comfortable being silly or goofy when the mood struck—ironic, considering silliness and goofiness had been trademarks of our *MPML* project. She was completely over the constant stream of negative comments. When people in the chat room started posting the address of Crazy Mocha online, revealing the location of the coffee shop where we spent so much of our time, it scared her. And the truth was, it scared me, too.

As she confided in me, as she explained that she went to sleep at night feeling as though the camera were still on her—even though it was all the way in my room—as she described the ways in which she no longer felt comfortable in her own home, I felt terrible, and I knew that things had to change. And when she explained her plans for the future, I felt incredibly sad, but I also understood. She had to make the right choices for her life. She had to do what was best for her.

Still, it was the end of an era. By the close of August 2007, Dez had moved out.

PIVOT

AFTER DEZ MOVED OUT, I RELOCATED TO A ONE-BEDROOM APARTMENT RIGHT NEXT DOOR TO FINISH OUT THE TERM OF MY LEASE. I'd never lived completely on my own before, and I missed her. I couldn't help feeling a bit lonely. Some of that loss was tempered, however, by the insane amount of traveling I was doing.

The culmination of everything I'd done thus far—the hosting gigs, live-streaming, and, especially, the "success" of the three-hundred-page iPhone bill video—was that agents and publicists and talent managers were starting to approach me right and left. I had known for months, ever since Macworld, really, that I eventually wanted to live on the West Coast. I also had a number of people in my life who were encouraging me to get to Los Angeles, specifically (since it's the center of the entertainment industry). So, I ended up taking a couple of meetings.

I wasn't sure what the upshot would be. It's not like I wanted to trade in my current job to become a Hollywood actress. I wasn't necessarily looking for a television show or a development deal, either; my focus was still online. I just wanted to get a sense of my options. Maybe a manager or a talent agent could create opportunities for me that I hadn't even dared to dream of at that time?

The more meetings I took, however, the more wary I became. I worried that I was either ripe to be taken advantage of (I knew nothing about Hollywood and some of these so-called managers seemed a little, well, shady) or in danger of signing with a traditional entertainment company that had no idea how to represent someone like me. The more agents I spoke with, the more I realized that Hollywood folks didn't understand what I was doing. Most of them didn't have a clue what I was about.

Generally speaking, online content creators like me do everything—lighting, filming, sound mixing, editing, and distributing via our online network—ourselves. There is no team of producers in place, no army of people working in different departments on your behalf. It's just you, and you're probably operating on a nonexistent budget. I figured the appeal of one day working in television would be to do a show that I *couldn't* produce myself, like a sitcom or a dramatic series. A few of the agents I met with (and at the time it was a *very* few) talked about getting me my "own show," by which they meant a reality series, but I didn't see the point of that—I already had a "show" about my life online. Most of the people I met with, however, didn't think my experience in front of the camera counted for much of anything. During a general meeting with one of the most well-known and well-respected firms in the business, a smartly dressed agent shook his head and said, "I'm not sure we can take you on as a client at this time. You just don't have enough television credits."

I was baffled. "Um, isn't that kind of why I'm here?" I asked. "So you can help me with that?"

A few weeks later, I was approached directly about being part of a national television ad campaign. This seemed like further confirmation that I didn't need a big, fancy agent. I decided to just keep doing what I'd always done—by myself, and on my own terms.

. . .

By mid- to late 2007, I was flying back and forth to the West Coast as often as two or three times a month. On the one hand, things were going quite well. For example, I traveled from San Francisco to L.A. with Justin to be interviewed by Kevin Sites for his *People of the Web* series.

Kevin Sites started reporting for Yahoo in 2005, after working for years as a freelance journalist, filing stories with most of the major news networks, including ABC, NBC, and CNN. He's considered one of the original "backpack journalists," someone who reports, shoots, edits, produces, and transmits his stories from the road, a kind of one-man news show, armed with only a backpack full of portable digital equipment. The style in which he works has been nicknamed the SoJo method, short for solo journalism—so, I could relate. He has reported from most major war zones and covered a slew of natural disasters. He's received numerous awards and accolades for his work. To be featured in his series, then, was kind of an honor.

I live-streamed during the entire interview (as did Justin), but as the three of us strolled around an outdoor mall in Santa Monica, a huge number of people in my chat room started making lewd comments about how I should head to the beach and prance around in a bikini. While I was being interviewed by an award-winning war correspondent. Great.

I'd started getting recognized in public—and not just in my hometown of Pittsburgh. I was standing outside Saddle Ranch, a kitschy country-western bar and grill on Sunset Boulevard, when someone approached me and asked to take a picture. I think that was the first time I'd ever been spotted outside of a tech conference or trade show, and it was surreal.

I had also started working more closely with the folks at TalkShoe, the podcasting company that hosted Leo's *net@night* and Shawn's *Geek*

Riot shows, which I had continued making appearances on or cohosting, respectively. By then I'd started my own show, too (broadcasting every Sunday at 8:45 p.m.), which functioned a little like a call-in radio program. Instead of dialing a landline and waiting for a radio producer to put you through to speak with a DJ, however, TalkShoe shows were basically giant conference calls—anyone who installed the software on their computer and registered for a TalkShoe account could be on the call, all at the same time (though I did have the ability to mute participants if things got too loud).

In my spare time (what little I had), in partnership with companies like TalkShoe, Viddler, and xTrain, I was hitting up every tech convention on the circuit, from the Podcast and New Media Expo to the Blog-World & New Media Expo to Photoshop World.

So, as I said, things were going pretty well. On the other hand, however, was the reality of what all that looked like behind the scenes. I still had no money and no representation. Though most of the companies I worked with covered my airfare from city to city, I was usually in charge of booking hotel accommodations myself. Obviously, I looked for the cheapest place I could find. I certainly wasn't staying in any fancy hotel suites.

During one such trip to San Francisco, I arrived at my hotel only to find that every light in the building was out. Was this some kind of citywide blackout? Nope. This was just my crummy hotel. There was no one at the front desk, either. Did this place close on the weekends? I have no idea. I think it was just that shady.

Justine Ezarik
@ijustine

+ Follow

En route to finding a new hotel. Longest night ever. :(

7:35 AM - 15 Jul 2007

I started immediately looking for other accommodations, but there were so many events going on in the area that every hotel I called was booked. Finally, stranded and pretty much out of options, I called one of the only people I knew in San Francisco, my friend Brian. We'd met a few months earlier online—because, if I haven't made it clear already, I meet virtually everyone I've ever known online—and he swung by to pick me up. Since I didn't know him very well at the time, I didn't take him up on his (very kind) offer to let me crash on his couch—meeting strangers from the Internet is one thing, but staying in their homes is not something I've ever been okay with—so we drove instead to a local twenty-four-hour Starbucks. He sat up the whole night with me, drinking coffee and talking, until the sun came up and I could figure out what to do.

I guess what I'm saying here is, my life at the time was anything but glamorous.

• • •

I was still in San Francisco when I decided to head to a book signing with Daniel Lyons, aka Fake Steve Jobs.

Daniel Lyons was a well-respected senior editor at *Forbes,* but in 2006 he started blogging—anonymously—as "Fake Steve Jobs." Just to give you an idea of the site's tone, the tagline was: "Dude, I invented the friggin' iPhone. Have you heard of it?" It was basically an entire website devoted to "Jobs" talking openly and honestly about how awesome and brilliant he was. It was hilarious. Speculation about who the site's author might be raged on for months; by early 2007, interest was so high that Bill Gates, in a rare joint appearance with Jobs, felt the need to joke that, no, he was *not* the one behind the blog.

By mid-2007, Lyons's true identity had been revealed, but he kept the site going. It was around that time that—still posing as Jobs—he started writing about me. In a post called "This Chick Is Getting Out of Hand," a response to a video I'd made in which I pretended to get the Apple logo tattooed on my back, he suggested that I had turned from fan to stalker. In response to another (albeit superweird) video created by a different female Apple fan, he wrote, "This Chick Scares Me Almost as Much as iJustine."

Fake Steve Jobs officially "hated" me. And it was great.

We sort of fell into a fun, playfully antagonistic relationship after that. In a blog post titled "My God I'm a Sexy Bitch," he posted a picture of "himself" and wrote several paragraphs about how good-looking he was and about the fact that women the world over couldn't help but be drawn to him. He ended the post with the truly wonderful line: "And hey, iJustine? You're welcome."

When Lyons eventually published a book version of the blog (with some additional info thrown in about the stock-options backdating scandal), called *Options: The Secret Life of Steve Jobs: A Parody,* I knew I'd make it a point to show up and get my autographed copy. Fake Steve Jobs was lovely and gracious and it was so much fun to finally meet him. We had a good laugh.

My first (and only) interaction with the real Steve Jobs did not go quite so well.

I was having lunch with a friend on the Apple campus in Cupertino. We were sitting in the cafeteria when I suddenly looked up to see that Steve Jobs—the *real* Steve Jobs—had just taken a seat at a table diagonal to me. I froze. I held my breath and sat stock-still and watched as he unloaded various Tupperware containers from his little brown paper bag, spread them out on the table, and prepared to eat.

I should point out here that my "obsession" with Steve Jobs had been pretty well documented by that point, and not just via the Fake Steve Jobs blog. Aside from talking about him on the Internet ad nauseam, aside from proudly displaying a framed photo of him on my desk, I'd also filmed a parody of the infamous "Leave Britney Alone" video by Chris Crocker—when the guy screamed and cried and wailed over the media's horrible treatment of Britney Spears after her failed "comeback" performance at the MTV Video Music Awards—called "Leave Steve Jobs Alone." With mascara streaking down my face, I screamed and cried and wailed, too. To the uninitiated, I no doubt looked like a complete and total crazy person.

Anyway, I'm sitting in the cafeteria in Cupertino, and I'm looking at Steve, and he's looking at me, and I realize he seems kind of panicked. Visions of all the silly photos, videos, tweets, and Steve-related content I'd posted over the years flashed before my eyes. Had he seen any of it? Was I on some kind of official watch list at Apple? Suddenly, he started shoving all of his little plastic containers back in his brown paper bag. I couldn't believe it. Steve Jobs was practically *running away* from me.

· · ·

Back home in Pittsburgh, I was still going strong with the live-stream. Sometimes it was actually fun, like the time I was hanging out in my room, listening to music, when someone from the chat room decided to call in to my local radio station and surprise me by requesting a song.

There were moments, too, when it was just weird: Like this one particular time I went home to visit my parents. I walked in the house and saw my father sitting at the kitchen table, watching television. Except he wasn't watching a TV show—he was watching a live feed of my backyard. Security cameras, you ask? Nope. He was deer-casting.

That would be me, running back and forth in front of my dad's infrared motion sensors, just making sure everything's functioning properly. You're welcome, Dad.

My father had taken several infrared cameras with motion sensors, hidden them in these little wooden structures that looked a bit like birdhouses, and mounted them in the woods behind our home—whenever a deer walked within range, the camera would automatically turn itself on and begin transmitting a signal to a receiver, which would in turn power on both the television and the VCR (in order to record the footage). And people think lifecasting is weird. I swear he had a more elaborate setup than I did.*

And then there were times when it was just plain hard. As people realized the influence they could have over my life—by prank call-

---

*He still fashions trail cameras to this day, in case you're wondering, sometimes using my old equipment—he'll take apart an old camera and add the infrared and motion sensors himself. You see, my dad is very handy. Also, if anyone out there wonders where my desire to lifecast came from, I would like to suggest that it is his fault.

ing, by having free drinks sent over to me and my friends in bars and restaurants (admittedly not the *worst* thing), by figuring out my location and spreading that info across the web—they started to grow ever more bold and aggressive.

Anthony, whom I was now calling "Skippy" because someone in the chat room had nicknamed him that and it stuck, was still appearing with some regularity on the feed, until one night when the viewers decided to "vote him off" my "show" like it was an episode of *Survivor*. There was really just one problem with that: the people on my live-stream weren't actors, they were my friends, and this wasn't actually a *show,* this was my life.

The more aggressive and unkind people on the Internet were toward those around me, the more I began to isolate myself. Of course, there were plenty of aggressive and unkind comments aimed at me, too. And let me tell you, constantly being judged for what you're doing, for what you're wearing, for how you speak or what you look like, will eventually take a toll. If my shorts were "too short," someone was sure to say something crass—without even realizing it, I had started wearing pants and long sleeves (rather than shorts and tank tops) when I was on camera. The pressure to entertain was enormous, and I was miserable.

I was starting to have "technical difficulties"—I'd turn the camera off and the immediate sense of relief was so cathartic, I'd suddenly be crying. Sleeping, too, became a kind of refuge, a chance for some peace and quiet. I started sleeping in longer and later—I just didn't see the point of waking up early, only to have to come up with some new way to entertain.

And then I experienced what was by far the scariest side effect of living my life online. I don't remember where I had been that evening, but I returned to my empty apartment to find the windows in my living room wide open. I didn't leave the windows in my house open, ever. I couldn't tell immediately if anything was missing—it's not like I had walked into an obvious crime scene—but I *knew* that someone had been inside. I was on the phone with Brian at the time, my friend from San Francisco who'd sat up with me in that all-night Starbucks.

"Oh my God, I think maybe I've been robbed?" I said, trembling. "I think someone broke into my apartment."

"What are you doing on the phone with me, then?" he yelled. "Hang up and call the cops!"

Which I did—and I locked myself in the bathroom, just in case someone *had* broken in and was still there. It was terrifying, and all at once I felt so incredibly powerless.

When the cops showed up, I explained about the windows being open, about some strange sounds I thought I had heard, about the fact that I had been scared and barricaded myself in the bathroom. They searched the apartment, but they didn't find anyone. They took notes, walked the perimeter of the building, radioed back to dispatch, until suddenly one of them turned and looked at me. "Wait a minute, are you the girl that's been live-streaming all the time?" he asked. "And you had that really big iPhone bill?"

"Yeah, that was me," I said.

And here is an example of one of the rare perks of live-streaming: the cops said they would do some extra patrolling in my neighborhood, just to make sure I was okay.

I didn't know which was worse: having the cops barge in unexpectedly because of a prank call, or calling them myself. What I did know was that I needed an indefinite break. I couldn't keep filming myself twenty-four hours a day. It just wasn't fun anymore. And as the year began drawing to a close, I realized I was done.

You wouldn't be crazy for saying, *Why do this at all? Why not just turn the camera off? No one was making you live-stream, so why are you whining? You brought this all on yourself.* On the surface, I can even understand that sentiment. But consider this: When Justin Kan went on the *Today* show to publicize the launch of Justin.tv, Ann Curry was notably skeptical. In fact, some people in the tech world have labeled the interview "cringe-worthy." She warned him (some would say sanctimoniously) about the "high price of fame." She referenced a critic who had publicly suggested that Justin might one day be embarrassed by what he had done. At one point she flat out admonished him: Why would a Yale graduate want to expose himself in this way?

But Justin wasn't trying to get famous. He wasn't trying to "expose" himself or get attention. He was trying to *build* something. And though it took a few years—Justin.tv would have to "pivot" several times (to use a tech industry start-up term)—he eventually found a sustainable market: Justin.tv became Twitch.tv, a live-streaming video game platform, which was acquired by Amazon in August 2014 for $970 million.

Not everyone will have that kind of success, of course (and I don't just mean financially), but when you're trying to build something you believe in, you don't stop when it gets tough. You don't give up. You don't just turn the camera off. You keep trying.

And I did keep trying—it's not like I never live-streamed again. I just knew I couldn't keep doing it every day, all day. It wasn't sustainable for me. I had to pivot. I had to keep going until I found something that worked.

iJUSTINE GOES WEST

SOMETIME AROUND THE END OF 2007, I WAS FINALLY READY TO MAKE THE MOVE TO THE WEST COAST. The transition to California, however, was a rough one.

I set my sights on San Francisco, rather than Los Angeles, for two main reasons: (1) L.A. might have been the center of the entertainment industry, but the Bay Area was home to the tech world; I figured that's where I'd be most comfortable, and where I'd most likely fit in. And (2) I actually knew some people in San Francisco, and by "some people" I mean Karen, my buddy from Jumpcut, and Brian, my all-night Starbucks friend. By chance, I'd met a group of guys in Pittsburgh who were getting ready to make the move, too, and they more or less offered to let me tag along. When the house they'd been eyeing fell through at the last minute, though, we ended up in a smaller apartment in Haight-Ashbury, the hipster section of the city—the birthplace, in fact, of hippie subculture.

I went out to California with a hideous pink suitcase, a pillow, and a lighting kit I'd stolen from the chiropractor's office. (Okay, I didn't *steal* it so much as *not return* it after finding it in the trunk of my car several days after I'd quit my job; seeing as how Dr. Rolex had called me worthless, I figured it was adequate severance pay.) That was pretty much it, though. I didn't have the money to take anything inconsequential. I just packed up what I could and headed out.

For the first few months, I slept on a cruddy old mattress—no box spring, no bed frame—shoved into the corner of the room. I had two whole blankets in my possession, so I usually wrapped one around the mattress to avoid infecting myself with Ebola or scabies or whatever might have been lurking deep within that old, stained-up fabric. When the huge clouds of marijuana smoke started wafting under my bedroom door, though, I realized I had a bigger problem. I had never even smoked a cigarette before, let alone weed, and these guys weren't just having an occasional joint to unwind in the evenings—I had unwittingly moved in with a group of hard-core stoners. Living in that apartment was like living inside a dry-ice machine. The constant stink of billowing weed smoke was making me physically ill—I slept with all the windows open and a blanket shoved underneath the door to my room. So now I was down to one blanket, and I was freezing. I only lasted a few months before moving out.

In the meantime, I'd been in contact with a couple of guys who had recently left their jobs at one of the video-sharing sites I had worked with to start an artist management company, specializing in YouTube and online talent. I was still resistant to the idea of signing with anyone, but I'd known these guys for a while. Besides, the fact that they both came from the digital world made me feel like I could trust them. Surely these two would be better able to understand my career than agents at a traditional Hollywood firm? So I agreed to give it a shot, but things didn't get much better. In fact, in terms of my living situation, they got worse.

Since I didn't have anywhere else to go, I relocated to L.A. to move in temporarily with one of my brand-new managers. At the time, it actually seemed like a perfectly fine arrangement—he was constantly on the road, almost never home, so I would have the house more or less to myself. I quickly started to feel trapped, though—I didn't know anyone. I didn't know the city very well. It was just me, by myself, in a big house, sitting around without a whole lot to do. The situation just didn't *feel* right, and it was slowly dawning on me that perhaps I had made a mistake.

When my manager finally took a break from traveling, I relocated again—this time to stay with the *other* manager . . . at his mom's house. Yes, you read that right. I moved in with my manager's mother and lived for a couple of months in her spare bedroom. She was incredibly sweet. She'd get up and putter around the kitchen in the mornings, making me breakfast. But the whole thing was obviously strange—stranger still because no one on my "team" seemed to think there was anything weird about this arrangement.

After a couple months of this nonsense, I realized I had to get out of there or else I was going to go crazy. By early autumn, I had a trip scheduled, a vacation I'd been looking forward to for weeks, and I figured it was now or never. I told my manager (and his mom) that I'd be out of town for a few days, but I packed up everything I had—about five suitcases' worth of stuff at the time—and never came back.

It would take a few years before I felt comfortable signing with another management firm. In the meantime, I went back to doing what had always seemed to work in the past—figuring things out by myself. I eventually found an apartment in Santa Monica. I was lucky in that I had made a few friends in the business, people who didn't mind helping me look over contracts and negotiate deals, people I trusted, who didn't ask for or take anything from me in return. And I learned a little something about trusting my gut and choosing my business partners wisely.

It's important for me to say that I don't think those first two managers were *bad* guys, by the way. It was still early days in terms of representing Internet talent, and back then, none of us really had any idea what we were doing, myself included. And like all seemingly negative experiences, some good things actually came out of it: my first two managers were instrumental in getting me to L.A. in the first place. They also introduced me to Brooke Brodack, aka Brookers, a rising Internet star they briefly represented, too.

• • •

I think it's pretty fair to say that I was a YouTube early adopter. After all, I was posting absurdist clips way back in 2006, months before I'd even heard of the *Yahoo! Talent Show* or met Alex Lindsay at PodCamp or been to Macworld for the first time. Brooke Brodack, however, was super early to the platform; by the time I'd uploaded six or seven videos, the *New Yorker* had already dubbed her "the first real YouTube star." She was twenty at the time, and YouTube had been around for only ten months. When we met, she had recently moved to L.A. from her home state of Massachusetts and signed a development deal with Carson Daly.

I figured hanging out with Brooke would be refreshing, that it would be wonderful to be around someone who truly understood what I'd been trying to build, who had been out there shooting and uploading videos to the web, just to see what could happen—just like me. And it *was* refreshing; mostly, though, it was fun. I think we were both pleasantly surprised to discover that we were just two weird chicks who happened to like the same things. Sometimes we made videos together. But more often than not, we'd sit around our manager's big, empty house in L.A. (where I was still crashing at the time) looking for something to do.

One night, bored as usual, we started watching Tom Green's show—*Tom Green's House Tonight*—the one he filmed from his very own living room and streamed live on the web. We watched his show with some regularity, actually, but when we realized that evening's guest was Carson Daly, we figured we might as well try to call in.

Obviously, I'd met Tom before, back in the *Yahoo! Talent Show* days, and Brooke, as I mentioned, had a deal going with Carson's production company. The number of mainstream stars trying to branch out into web-based entertainment was so small at the time, though, that I'd recently had a chance to work with Carson, too. He was an investor in a social networking start-up called ChannelMe.tv, for which I'd been hired as a kind of spokesperson. Over the course of several months, I filmed a number of videos for the site, including one in which Carson sent me on a "secret mission" to "build an online community" set to a kind of *Mission: Impossible*–style tune.

Anyway, since this was a web series, Brooke and I had called in via Skype—Tom had a computer sitting on the side of his desk, and our faces were now prominently filling the screen. Not everyone really understood what was going on, though. Andrew Dice Clay was Tom's other guest that night, and he didn't just *not* know who Brooke and I were, he seemed baffled by the entire concept of the Internet.

"Who is this girl that's waving?" he said finally, gesturing to the computer.

"That's iJustine. I know that girl," Carson said by way of explanation. "And Brookers."

There's a brief moment when everyone sort of starts talking over each other, trying to explain who Brooke and I are and why we're suddenly on Tom Green's show, but it takes Clay a few minutes to grasp that we aren't just heads in a box, that Brooke and I are actually listening to the live broadcast via the web.

"Oh, they're *hearin'* us," he says, in that heavy Brooklyn accent he's famous for, before turning to Tom. "Oh, this is that thing you started. The invention."

There's another outburst of chatter, mostly about the Internet in general—Carson asks Brooke and me where we're calling from—but when Clay suddenly realizes he can communicate directly with the two of us, he completely changes tack. "What are you, a dancer?" he asks me. "What do you do?"

"Am I a dancer?" I ask, incredulous. "Uh, no . . . are *you* a dancer?"

At this point, Carson jumps in to try to explain, again, who Brooke and I are, that we're pretty well known for making videos on the web—that he's done some work with us, in fact. He goes on to describe the ways in which he's fascinated by what's now possible online. And that's when Clay gets excited. "Dis is something he can make money from, I'm tellin' ya," he says to Carson, while pointing directly at Tom's computer. At the time, I wasn't sure if the "this" he was referring to was the computer, the Internet in general, or VoIP technology, but he continued: "*This* thing? He had it last time . . . where there's *people* in there . . . that you can actually talk to!"

Tom had to explain that, while he might be considered a kind of pioneer in terms of producing mainstream-style content for the web, he didn't actually *invent* the Internet. Or Skype. It was amazing. The whole thing reminded me of that scene from *Zoolander* when Owen Wilson's character is just blown away to discover that the secret files he's looking for are, literally, *in the computer*.

· · ·

So, I was officially living on the West Coast, and as 2007 bled into 2008, I was still doing a lot of the same sorts of things—partnering with emerging tech and social media companies and attending tech shows and trade conferences, mostly. Karen and I returned to Macworld that January (this time we decided we wanted to be first through the doors, so we camped out outside the convention hall as if waiting for another iPhone launch). By March, I was headed down to Austin for my first trip to South by Southwest.

I think most people know SXSW either as a music festival (which, despite becoming extremely popular in recent years, has actually been around since the eighties, launching the careers of artists like Hanson, John Mayer, James Blunt, and Katy Perry), or a film festival (the film component was added back in 1994), but it's also got an "interactive" element, too. Every year, people from around the country flock down to Texas to check out the latest in gaming and gadgets, as well as attend panels with top Internet and tech entrepreneurs. In fact, it was at the 2007 conference that the founders of Twitter, then still very much a fledgling site with middling traffic, made some supersmart marketing moves, including setting up a couple giant plasma screens in the hallways of the Austin Convention Center, on which they streamed nothing but tweets from festivalgoers. It proved to be the site's tipping point, and usage exploded, skyrocketing from an average of twenty thousand messages a day (across the entire network) to more than sixty thousand. By the end of the week, Twitter had won the SXSW Web Award (in the blog category). By April, *Newsweek* had published an article titled "Twitter: Is Brevity the Next Big Thing?" And by March 2008, around the time I was headed down to Texas, the site had grown to more than a million total users and was averaging 3 million tweets a day. Which sounds like a lot, except, hold on—we'll come back to that in a minute.

I was in town with the crew from Viddler, promoting their video-sharing site as well as their "Brand Yourself" campaign. We made some videos and hit up the panels—the year's big news was that Mark Zuckerberg, the creator of Facebook, was delivering the keynote speech. During the second half of the festival, though, when the tech portion more or less ends and the music portion takes over, I thought it would be fun to do some man-on-the-street-style interviews. I wanted to see if these die-hard music fans knew anything about the tech portion of the conference. (Spoiler alert: they did not.) Here are some of my favorite results from that unexpectedly hilarious question-and-answer session:

Q: Did you check out Mark Zuckerberg's keynote speech?

A: I don't know what you're talking about.

A: Everyone keeps talking about Mark Zuckerberg. Who is that? He's alt-country, right?

A: Does he have a demo?

Q: Have you heard of Twitter?

A: I haven't.

A: No.

A: *Juner?**

Q: Did you hear they released the iPhone SDK?

A: I don't know what that means. That's just letters.

Obviously I wasn't having a lot of success with the tech questions, so I briefly decided to ask about video games. Since this was a music crowd, I figured everyone would be familiar with Rock Band (essentially the sequel to the wildly popular Guitar Hero series). Here's how *that* went:

Q: So, Rock Band. What level are you? Hard? Expert?

A: Uh, I don't know. . . . We're indie right now?

And now for my personal favorite:

---

*See what I mean? Three million tweets a day, and most people I spoke with still hadn't heard of it.

Q: Say a lot of people started visiting your website. How would you deal with the scaling of your infrastructure?

A: Uh, I wouldn't. I'd just chill.

It's worth mentioning, by the way, that had any of these people turned the tables and asked *me* a question about music, I would have failed miserably. I knew nothing about the music industry; I knew even less about emerging or underground artists. I just couldn't help but giggle when the guy asked where he could find Mark Zuckerberg's demo tape.

. . .

With the live-stream largely done (I'd still stream occasionally, either as part of my weekly podcast or for the heck of it, but I was down to a couple hours a week) I returned to making funny videos, something I hadn't done with any real consistency in months. The only difference was that now—in contrast to the "early days," that period back in 2006, before I'd entered the *Yahoo! Talent Show*—my online network had grown considerably. It's hard to be exact, but my best estimate is that I had amassed fifty thousand Myspace friends, I was probably hovering somewhere around twenty to fifty thousand YouTube subscribers, and I'd long ago hit my five-thousand-friend limit on Facebook.

In April, I filmed my first music video, a spoof on the Madonna/Justin Timberlake collaboration "4 Minutes." It was common practice in those days—actually, it's still common practice—for me to make up words while singing along to the radio, because I never knew what the real words were, anyway. At some point, it seemed like a concept that might work on YouTube, so I changed the urgent, social-awareness lyrics of "4 Minutes" to an urgent, personal awareness of just how long it usually took me to download an episode of *Lost* (one of my favorite shows) to iTunes on FiOS: *Come on, store, I'm waiting for my new download to go / Well, I don't have time, you will be mine, wanna play my new show.*

That clip has been viewed nearly a million times. And, yes, I'm embarrassed just typing those ridiculous lyrics.

I kept going with the music videos for a while, continuing to film spoofs of greater and greater extravagance, like the Black Eyed Peas hit "I Gotta Feeling" (more than 15 million views), which was altered from a song about the impending awesomeness of a night out with friends to the impending awesomeness of the new profile pic that was sure to result from a night out with friends. Or Shakira's "She Wolf," in which I changed the chorus to ask, "What the hell is a she wolf?" (Because, seriously, what the hell is it?) To this day, they're still some of the most-watched videos I've ever produced, despite working with rudimentary equipment: the camera I used for "I Gotta Feeling" was a Canon point-and-shoot; my green screen was an IKEA blanket tacked up to the wall in my room.

By July, the second-generation iPhone—the 3G—had been released. I'd had every intention of going to an Apple Store in North Carolina, where I was vacationing with my family, to cover the launch, until I realized that the closest one was more than three hours away from our beach rental. As an alternative, I thought I'd try to buy one at a local

AT&T outlet, until I realized the one I'd been planning on visiting was not, in fact, a *store*. Fail #2. Back home in California, nearly a week after the launch, I called more than thirty-five Apple Stores in search of a phone, only to discover that every single store was out of stock. The resulting video, "THE WORLD IS OUT OF IPHONES!!!!!"—in which an Apple employee told me that Steve Jobs was "a big butthead," in response to my question "Why is he doing this?"—landed on the Yahoo home page.

By August, I'd filmed my "I WANT A CHEESEBURGER" rant, which hit six hundred thousand views inside of a week.

It wasn't just me out there, either, making strange videos seemingly about nothing and racking up huge numbers of views online—by mid-2008, there was suddenly a growing crop of YouTube "stars." Being "famous on the Internet" had become, well, a *thing*. As a result, major corporations—not just tech start-ups, but the GEs and Fords and Intels of the world—had started hiring Internet personalities as spokespeople. Web stars were starting, slowly, to cross over. And with that sudden increase of attention came what I might call the first major wave of backlash from cultural critics and writers and reporters in the mainstream press. A number of articles were published about me during this period, some written with barely disguised snark, others with out-and-out disdain, describing my "popularity" as both inexplicable and unearned. It was during this time that a reputable tech publication labeled me a "bug-eyed, squealing" enthusiast. A popular Manhattan-based blog ran a piece called "Pretty Girls Becoming Popular Online: What Does It Mean?" in which they referred to the people who watched my videos or subscribed to my channels as "mindless lemmings." It seemed like a growing and vocal contingent of people were openly rooting for folks like me to fail.

Let's talk about that for a minute, shall we?

Roughly nine months or so after the "300-page iPhone bill" video went viral, I was hired by AT&T to film a reality web series called *Lost in America*. The premise was that I would travel to various cities across the U.S.—Anchorage, Austin, Chicago—where I'd have to solve "missions" or "mysteries" using only my mobile phone, a Samsung Black-Jack II. Bonus: Karen Nguyen would be my costar.

I loved the whole experience—who wouldn't love getting paid to travel the country with one of their closest friends? The show gave me another chance to work with the guys at Studio 8, a hilarious comedy website that had evolved into a full-blown production studio, specializing in creating online video content. (I had filmed the Carson Daly video with the Studio 8 guys, too.) I also got a chance to meet and work with Drew Baldwin—he was the guy doling out the "missions" to Karen and me on camera—who would go on to cofound a company called Tubefilter, which operates the Streamy Awards. (Seriously: Internet? Very small world.) We shot somewhere in the neighborhood of ten or eleven episodes, all of which were distributed on the mini-site ATTLostinAmerica.com.

Within two weeks of the show's debut, however, *Advertising Age* ran a story about the apparent failure of the whole project: "AT&T's iJustine Web Series Doesn't Exactly Go Viral: YouTube Stars as Spokesmodels May Not Be Such a Great Idea After All."

Oh, man. It's just positively gleeful, right? I mean, that headline is dripping with sarcasm. The article goes on to suggest that the show garnered around thirty thousand views across multiple social media platforms, including Myspace and YouTube (though the reporter didn't have access to the analytics from AT&T's mini-site). Since the clips I posted on my own channels often received many, many more views than that, the reporter from *Ad Age* interpreted that the show hadn't been particularly successful. He extrapolated further that hiring YouTube talent was, basically, a giant waste of time.

The thing is, I would've been fine with it if the point of the article was that the reporter just didn't like me or didn't like the show—I'd been doing this long enough to know that you can't please everybody. What he was suggesting, however, was that because the show didn't go "viral," it wasn't successful. It's a viewpoint that represents a complete lack of familiarity with Internet distribution channels. It's also a total misrepresentation of how the web works. Here's why:

Karen and I were hired solely as on-air talent—it wasn't our job to blog or tweet about the show, or to upload promotional spots to YouTube. In other words, we weren't hired as *distribution avenues*; we were hired to show up and deliver some lines. Most of us involved with *Lost in America* tweeted and blogged about it anyway, if for no other reason than that we were proud of our work. I posted a few behind-the-scenes-style vlogs on YouTube as well, because I figured my followers would be curious to know what I'd been up to and why I was traveling so much. Those videos, which weren't mentioned in the article, pulled in somewhere around 120,000 views. Had the intention of the show been to create something viral—forgetting for a minute the fact that an eight- or ten-minute-long video is unlikely to go viral in any context—AT&T would have paid for the use of our online network. The point of the show, however, was to drive traffic to AT&T's mini-site, which it did.

If you're wondering why any of this matters *now,* it's because corporate America is still trying to figure out this whole Internet thing nearly a decade later. Frantic articles keep getting published about the fact that, among American teenagers, Internet personalities are more recognizable and more influential than even the biggest Hollywood celebrities—but when actor and comedian Kevin Hart asked to be compensated to tap into his personal social network to promote a movie, a studio executive (in a private email that was later made public in the 2014 data hack of Sony Pictures) called him a "whore."

I get it when people say, "How hard is it to send a tweet?" What I think people sometimes fail to understand about amassing a following online, though, is that if you want to build an engaged audience (and Kevin Hart, by the way, has nearly 17 million Twitter followers), you have to provide consistent content—whether that's makeup tutorials, music video spoofs, absurdist comedy sketches, or clips about dancing in Apple Stores, you have to be true to your brand. What you can't do is spam your own accounts. It's why I posted two episodes of *Lost in America* to YouTube, and *only* two—any more than that would've felt like I was clogging my channel with promotional material, which isn't what my subscribers signed up for. The minute someone like me stops creating consistent, reliable content, they'll start to lose their audience. I imagine that's what Kevin Hart meant when he said publicly, in response to the insult from the Sony exec, that he was "protecting his brand." It's the reason I've turned down lots of jobs over the years—I refuse to give up control over what I post on my own accounts. To an outsider looking in, it might be hard to understand why more than 7 million people would watch a video of a girl explaining her trouble trying to order a cheeseburger, but that doesn't mean that my followers—anyone's followers—are mindless lemmings. It doesn't mean their loyalty is fickle. On the contrary, that audience took years and years to build. Losing that audience, on the other hand, can happen much, much quicker.

I mean, if it were that easy, everyone on Twitter would have an audience of millions.

. . .

Of course, not everything I've worked on has been successful. In fact, a number of projects I signed up for turned out to be—in 2008—a little ahead of their time. For example, I was hired to host a biweekly music video show on a new platform called PluggedIn.com* (despite the fact that, as previously mentioned, I knew nothing about music; I swear I took the job because someone said I'd get a chance to meet Will Smith—his company provided venture funding for the site—but that never happened). PluggedIn was supposed to become the Hulu for HD music videos—but it never quite took off. I'm not sure the resources were there, or that the company could afford the necessary bandwidth.

I was also a huge supporter of a site called DailyBooth, where users could upload a daily photo and receive comments—it was not unlike YouTube, albeit with less barrier to entry because you didn't have to shoot and edit a video. I felt about DailyBooth in 2008 the way I felt about Twitter in 2006; I was sure it would take off—but it never did. Instagram, however, launched two years later, at the end of 2010, and exploded.

I'd even argue that AT&T's *Lost in America* was a little too early, in

---

*This was a completely separate venture from the current iteration of PluggedIn, which is owned by the socially conservative group Focus on the Family.

that people weren't yet consuming content the way they do now, without distinguishing between shows that were made to air on television and content that was created explicitly for the web.

By the end of that year, however, another shift was occurring on the Internet landscape. The gap between the online world and mainstream entertainment was slowly starting to close.

GOING MAINSTREAM

**YOUTUBE WAS SUCCESSFUL PRETTY MUCH RIGHT FROM THE START, GROW-
ING QUICKLY AND STEADILY FOLLOWING ITS LAUNCH IN 2005 TO BECOME,
FAR AND AWAY, THE MOST POPULAR VIDEO-SHARING SITE ON THE WEB.**
But 2009 was a watershed year—the platform, now the fourth most
popular site on the entire Internet, was exceeding a billion views a day,
changing the way we consumed content. Not only were more people
watching videos online but they were watching those videos for longer
periods of time. More people were creating and uploading their own
original content, too. By the middle of that year, President Obama had
launched his own channel. So had the pope.

As a result of this growth, YouTube began courting the content
providers that had helped to make the site so popular in the first place.
(Even though music videos received the most views, content creators
like me had the most-subscribed-to channels, which makes sense when
you think about it—we're constantly churning out new clips, often on a
near-daily basis; by contrast, pop stars might release, at most, three or
four music videos every year.) One way to do this was to allow us a share
of the ad revenue; I'd been a member of the Partner Program since 2007,

the year of its inception. Another was to help drive traffic to certain channels by promoting "featured" videos on the YouTube home page—it was in YouTube's interest, in other words, for its native content creators to do well. So whereas I had once focused my attention on sites like Revver and Viddler, I began to think of YouTube as a more primary destination, kind of like a home base. The more traffic increased to the site as a whole (and, downstream, to our videos in particular), the more revenue content creators like me received. For the first time, I had some real financial stability. On YouTube, I could suddenly make a decent living.

Despite this bustling new economy, most of us were working independently of one another. Brookers—by virtue of the fact that we were briefly represented by the same firm (at a time when very few managers were taking on Internet talent)—was one of the only people I'd met who was out there doing the same thing I'd been doing. But that was about to change, too. YouTube, in an attempt to keep growing its business, was getting ready to take on the traditional television industry. One of the first major attempts to do that was YouTube Live.

It was billed as "part concert, part variety show, and part party"; the event—streamed live on YouTube from Fort Mason in San Francisco—opened and closed with performances by Katy Perry and Akon, respectively, but it featured lots of online stars in between, including people like Tay Zonday, creator of the wildly popular "Chocolate Rain" video (remember that? The young, bespectacled guy with the unbelievably deep voice?), and Aaron Yonda and Matt Sloan, the duo behind *Chad Vader: Day Shift Manager* (a *Star Wars* parody in which the title character worked as a manager of a grocery store called Empire Market). Presenters ranged from will.i.am to the "Will It Blend?" guy. There were also all these weird and unlikely stage pairings—funtwo, a South Korean amateur guitar player (whose cover of "Canon Rock" went viral after someone *else* posted the clip to YouTube), got to play a mini-concert with Joe Satriani, one of the greatest guitar players in the world, a virtuoso who's sold 10 million albums and toured with people like Mick Jagger. I mean, how crazy is that?

As for me, I didn't have any onstage bits to perform, but I *did* get a pretty cool ride to the party. Since Virgin America airlines launched in 2007, Richard Branson's company has made it a point to reach out to tech and online folks (a pretty solid marketing strategy, since his is the only airline based out of San Francisco). Earlier that summer, just a few months before YouTube Live, in fact, I'd been invited to cover the unveiling of Virgin Galactic WhiteKnightTwo, the first commercial space shuttle, for my YouTube channel. (Branson has been at the forefront of "space tourism," which would give regular—albeit *extremely* wealthy—folks the chance to fly into outer space.) By fall, Virgin became the first American airline to offer in-flight Wi-Fi fleet-wide. To publicize this, Virgin sent up a plane to circle the skies of San Francisco packed with reporters and bloggers (including yours truly), all of whom were given a chance to try out the service. Keith Powell and Katrina Bowden from *30 Rock* were on hand to star in a small skit, which was beamed down to YouTube Live—the first ever air-to-ground video stream—from thirty-five thousand feet. After landing, we all headed over to Fort Mason to join the show.

More than just a first foray into webcasting, YouTube Live was by far the biggest thing the site had ever attempted to pull off; for most of us content creators, it was also the first chance we'd had to actually meet each other in person. Truthfully, I think many of us were less excited about seeing the celebrity performers up close than we were about the chance to hang out with each other.

Of course, none of that means the show was considered a commercial or critical success (no matter how awesome *I* thought it was)—viewership peaked at around seven hundred thousand, a small audience by television standards, and what was supposed to be an annual event has actually never happened again. (In 2013, the site hosted the YouTube Music Awards, but they're still trying to get the formula right on that event, too.) What YouTube Live accomplished, however, was to demonstrate the site's commitment to fostering its native talent. It helped bridge the gap between the online and mainstream entertainment worlds. What had once seemingly been a site for one-hit-wonder-type viral sensations was quickly becoming a legitimate launching point for a career in Hollywood. And there is no more obvious example of that than the case of Justin Bieber—2009 was the year the biggest sensation to come out of the web would cross over.

Justine Ezarik 🐦   +👤 Follow
@ijustine

Wow, just found @justinbieber on youtube (and twitter). He's really talented! http://bit.ly /2op96k

↩ ⟲ ★ ⋯
12:54 PM - 4 Sep 2009

Most people know that Justin Bieber was discovered on YouTube (in 2007), and that he's been wildly, ridiculously, improbably successful—with his first EP, he became the first artist in history to have seven different songs from a debut album reach the *Billboard* Hot 100; to date, he's sold more than 15 million albums. What's particularly interesting about his career, though, is the fact that he's managed to stay ahead of the curve when it comes to tech trends: he's amazingly adept in the world of social media; as I write this, he's the second most popular person on Twitter, with nearly 61 million followers. The premiere of his 2011 documentary, *Never Say Never* (which I got to cover with former MTV VJ Quddus), was one of the first to be live-streamed to the web. And he doesn't just *use* the latest social media platforms, he's also, apparently, a pretty savvy investor within the start-up world; it's been reported that he owns stakes of Stamped, Spotify, and a slew of other companies. In 2012, he was on the cover of *Forbes*.

It's also worth pointing out his age: the Biebs was only fifteen when his first album came out; it's possible that having a correspondingly young audience only contributed to his success. After all, teenagers have always been trendsetters and tastemakers; it's young people who determine what's cool and in fashion. But it's thanks to sites like YouTube that teenagers are more connected than ever. For the first time in history, it's possible for teens to influence each other on a *global* scale.

. . .

YouTube wasn't the only example of the ways in which online and traditional entertainment were merging—by 2009, Twitter had also gone mainstream. Celebrities were joining in droves what had once been the domain of techies and early adopters; and a lot of that, believe it or not, had to do with Ashton Kutcher.

You may remember Ashton's very public campaign to become the first Twitter user to attract a million followers—which he did, in April 2009. But the backstory of how and why that happened—which goes way beyond a desire to be "popular" on the web—is, I think, way more interesting.

Ashton joined Twitter in 2009, at a time when he was most famous for playing a dopey kid on *That '70s Show,* as well as for hosting MTV's *Punk'd*—unless, of course, you're me, in which case you know him best from that time you inadvertently created a fake Myspace profile and people thought you *were* him for a while. (So awkward. . . .) Anyway, let me give you some context here: January 2009 was nearly a year after my first trip to SXSW—despite the site's average of 3 million tweets a day, most of the people I spoke with on the streets of Austin hadn't even heard of it yet. It had been more than two years since Twitter's so-called tipping point (also at SXSW), when the site first started to gain traction within the tech community. In all that time, even while growing steadily, it still hadn't *really* taken off yet. By late 2008/early 2009, very few celebrities had joined (Lady Gaga and Britney Spears were early to the site, in March and October 2008, respectively), and no one had amassed a million followers.

Even before sending out his very first tweet, Ashton had quietly been learning about the web and the ways in which traditional entertainment, advertising, and social media were converging. Along with the partners in his production company, Katalyst, he'd started experimenting within the space: taking meetings with tech entrepreneurs, hiring some digital experts, and producing some web-only content (namely, an animated series called *Blah Girls*). After joining Twitter and quickly amassing a following of 750,000 in just a few months—easily making his one of the most popular accounts on the entire site—he decided to test his sphere of influence. He partnered with Malaria No More, a nonprofit organization with the goal of ending malaria-related deaths in Africa, and started tweeting social-awareness messages. And that's when the idea for the one-million-follower contest came about.

Ashton and his team challenged CNN, whose *Breaking News* Twitter feed was the second most popular account at the time, to a race to a million followers (via a video posted on Qik, naturally), set a deadline, and launched a very high-profile campaign, promising to donate ten thousand malarial nets upon winning. As the race heated up, CNN promised to match that donation if they won, and the network's most popular anchors, including Anderson Cooper and Wolf Blitzer, started hyping the contest on TV. At some point, the thing was so pervasive that as I was driving around Pittsburgh, home for a few days to visit family, I saw a "Follow Ashton Kutcher on Twitter" billboard on the side of the road. (As it turns out, one of the largest billboard companies in the country offered to put them up—in states all over the U.S.—pro bono.)

When the contest ended, Ashton had won—and he remained the most-followed Twitter user for a while (with roughly 16 million followers, he now hovers somewhere within the top fifty). Within the week, he went on *Oprah* and helped the host send her first tweet. Not surprisingly, Twitter exploded—what actor, musician, political figure, or Internet personality doesn't have a Twitter account these days?—and Ashton was now firmly implanted in the digital space.

• • •

In the summer of 2009, my sisters, Breanne and Jenna, were visiting me in L.A. when we decided to embark on a totally spontaneous road trip to Vegas. *So* spontaneous, in fact, that my father, who knew I didn't so much as know how to change a flat, pleaded with me to at least get the air in my tires checked before hitting the road. We didn't. We did, however, find a very nice man from AAA working on someone else's car in a Starbucks parking lot—obviously, our first stop—so I flashed him my membership card and shot a quick video while he took care of business. Mission accomplished.

At some point during that drive, I tweeted that I was en route to

Vegas. (By the way, it's worth mentioning that my sister was doing the actual driving. Please do not drive and tweet!!) Less than an hour later, I got an unexpected response: a press rep associated with Ashton's new film, *Spread*—which just so happened to be premiering that week at the Palms—asked if I was interested in interviewing him for my YouTube channel. Obviously I said yes.

By then I'd had an opportunity to rub shoulders with some celebs in various work-related circumstances—I'd met Akon at YouTube Live, I'd interviewed a few people at SXSW, I'd been a pseudo–red carpet reporter at the premiere of *Get Smart* (as part of a promotional thing with Cadillac)—but I hadn't done a ton of correspondent work. So, when I met Ashton, I asked him a few obligatory questions about his movie, but I was far more interested in talking about the Internet. I wanted to know which Twitter apps he preferred, if he was following me (*hello*); we talked a little about the one-million-follower campaign. Even after the camera was off (obviously I filmed the interview), we chatted a bit longer about apps and start-ups and some friends we wound up having in common.

Since that interview, Ashton has gone on to become a wildly successful venture capitalist; he's invested in a slew of start-ups, including Skype, Foursquare, and Airbnb. And because the Internet is a very, *very* small world, we've had the opportunity to work together several times, on another Malaria No More campaign, on a web-only advertisement for Popchips (another company in which he's an investor; we Punk'd the staffers at TMZ), and a video to promote the web launch of his show *The Beautiful Life: TBL*. Mostly, though, I've enjoyed seeing what he's managed to do in the tech world: he's been a creative director for Ooma (an Internet-based phone company) and was named a product engineer at Lenovo, where he was instrumental in designing the Yoga 2 tablet.

Ashton and me goofing around on the set of his 2011 film No Strings Attached. *I filmed a small cameo, and then they went ahead and cut that scene right out of the movie. I will assume that had more to do with Ashton's outfit (what is he wearing?) than my acting abilities.*

I think a lot of people probably doubted him—the announcement of his role as a product engineer, in particular, was met with a bit of suspicion and some outright snickering—but he is someone who really gets it, a passionate person who's managed to cross over from Hollywood to the tech space, paving the way for others—through his (relatively) early adoption of Twitter and his embrace of digital marketing—to do the same, as well as for those in the tech space to cross over into Hollywood. He had an interest, educated himself, and went for it, regardless of the naysayers. In my book (and not just figuratively speaking), that makes him a pretty cool dude.

• • •

As the lines between online and mainstream content and culture continued to blur, more and more opportunities came my way, including a chance to report from the red carpet at the MTV Movie Awards and a gig as the first official "Twitter correspondent" for the MTV VMAs several months later. The year 2009 was also when I got my first real "acting" job—despite the fact that I still didn't have representation, I landed a small role on *Law & Order: SVU.*

If you're wondering how to go about getting a job on TV when you don't have an agent, by the way, you could always do what I did, which is just tweet the casting director. *Law & Order* had long been one of my favorite shows (I binge-watch on Netflix, naturally)—and *SVU* is easily the best spin-off of the entire franchise, no question—so when I saw the name Jonathan Strauss pop up in the credits, I figured I might as well reach out. Just to let him know that if he ever needed someone to play a victim, I was willing. *Totally normal.* (Right?)

Justine Ezarik
@ijustine

+⚫ Follow

@JSCasting can I be in an episode of Law and Order SVU? Please! I swear I'd make the best victim ever!! I'll also make you cookies.

3:09 PM - 25 Jul 2009

Anyway, after I don't know how many unsolicited tweets, I reached out to Jonathan a final time; I had to be in New York (for the VMAs, incidentally) and I asked if he might be willing to meet. Amazingly, he said yes. The visit was short and sweet, and he told me he'd let me know when and if they had a script for me to read—I figured I wouldn't hear from him for months, if ever. But a week later, he called: Did I want to play the role of a young woman who gets strangled to death in her hotel room in the first few minutes of an episode? Um, *yes.*

As amazing as it was to work with actors like Mariska Hargitay and Christopher Meloni on one of the most iconic shows in the history of television (although, to say I "worked" with them might be a bit of a stretch—I was pretending to be dead by the time either of them made it on-screen), and as much as I got a kick out of sitting in the makeup chair and being made to look like a corpse (complete with a Y-shaped row of stitches across my chest, post-autopsy), the best part of the entire experience was easily the backstage access granted to me by the producers. Despite the fact that they'd never really allowed someone to film a behind-the-scenes video from the set—and the producers had to jump through all kinds of hoops to secure approval—I was allowed to document just about anything I wanted, and to share that footage with my friends and followers online. And I took my camera everywhere: to the wardrobe department, inside a courtroom holding cell (while wearing a bathrobe, which was my costume for a large part of the episode), on board the catering truck, *everywhere*. Rather than being standoffish or avoiding the intrusion altogether, everyone in the cast was eager to make an appearance; in fact, Ice-T and Richard Belzer didn't just say "hi" to the camera, they gave out their Twitter handles. For the better part of the shoot, I was known primarily as "the Twitter girl."

In the meantime, I continued doing what I'd always done: making videos, uploading them to the web, coming up with new ways to (hopefully) engage with my audience. I started *Ask iJ,* an ongoing video series in which I respond to questions I receive on Facebook, Twitter, YouTube, and my personal blog (shout out to Geoff Smith, an amazingly talented musician, jingle writer, and podcaster, who composed the ridiculously catchy *Ask iJ* theme song!).

173

Nothing lasts forever, though, especially not on the Internet, and 2009 brought about some sad changes, too—Yahoo, three years after acquiring Jumpcut, finally decided to fold the site. It was tough on Karen and her coworkers, and it was bittersweet even for me. The Jumpcut team had taken me in and become some of my first real friends in the business; I'd used the site's technology for years. I was such a devotee of the company, in fact, that I once went on a date with it.

Seriously. Sort of.

Someone in our group—I no longer remember who—thought it would be funny to film a romantic outing between me and, well, the website, so Karen and I and the rest of the crew spent a couple hours blowing up and printing out a life-sized Jumpcut logo and turning it into a sandwich-board-style costume. In the video, I nervously prepare for the big date in my hotel room, take an elevator downstairs to meet my date in the lobby, and then the two of us go out for a candlelit dinner. Is it weird that that's one of the better dates I've been on?

• • •

After the boom of 2009, I had more stability than I'd ever had in my adult life, but it's not as if all the pressure went away; it's not like I could rest easy. I certainly didn't feel like I had "made it." The job of a content creator is a nonstop, 24/7 kind of gig—no matter how many videos you've made, no matter how successful those videos may have been, you still have to keep churning out new material, which may or may not be well received. What was popular last month may not be popular this month. The more new people crop up online, the more you may find yourself competing for views. I was, however, more confident

The date started out so well, but then Jumpcut drank too much and needed help getting home. Typical.

Vintage iJustine video: Date with Jumpcut

than ever, more convinced that I could achieve pretty much whatever I wanted. And by 2010 I had a new goal in mind.

One year earlier, Karen and I had returned, for the third year in a row, to Macworld. It was the last year that Apple would participate in the expo, and Steve Jobs had announced that he wouldn't be there to deliver the keynote speech—Philip Schiller, Apple's senior vice president of worldwide marketing, would do that for him. Rumors about Steve's health had swirled for months, but the truth of his condition was still largely a secret. He was skipping the trade show, according to a letter posted to the Apple website, due to a "hormone imbalance."

In his absence, Karen and I launched "Real World News with iJustine and Karen," a hard-hitting, investigative (single episode) series wherein we reported on various unconfirmed rumors of Steve Jobs sightings. For the video, we slapped an image of Jobs's face on a column outside the Moscone Center, tacked a black, long-sleeved shirt underneath it, and then—intrepid journalist that I was—I proceeded to score the only on-camera interview with him of the entire conference. I held the microphone up to a 2-D image of his face and, after asking each question, waited patiently for his (very, very quiet . . . some might say impossible-to-hear) response.

When I sent it back over to Karen, she called it "an exclusive, fantastic interview." She promised that we'd return with more news. At that point, you can hear me, positioned just off camera, whispering, "And stuff," prodding Karen to be sillier, more outrageous, just like I'd prodded Dez all those years before.

"And stuff," Karen said. "More news . . . and stuff." A moment later, something occurred to her. "Why wasn't he wearing pants?" she asked, straight to camera. "Why didn't you ask him *that*?"

Here's Steve Jobs telling me how impressed he is with my reporting skills.

A year later, the first-generation iPad was launching (during a special event on the Cupertino campus) and I was more determined than ever—I was going to be part of the press. Once again, Jobs was giving the keynote speech, and the anticipation was more frenzied than it had been even for the launch of the iPhone; according to the *Wall Street Journal,* "the last time there was this much excitement about a tablet it had some commandments on it." And once again, I didn't have a pass to get in the actual room.

What I had, however, was a friend who worked at Apple, so I took *his* pass and snuck in. Jobs had just finished his keynote, and they'd begun opening the room up for reporters and bloggers. I filed in with the rest of the journalists, badge in hand, and there it was—the first Apple iPad. I filmed as much as I could until someone came up behind me and tapped me on the shoulder.

"Are you iJustine?"

"Yes!" I shouted, probably a little too loudly. I was so pumped about the release of the iPad, and now someone at the launch had recognized me. I was at Apple and they knew who I was! *These people know who I am!* I thought.

And then I realized I had been "recognized" by security. I wasn't on Apple's approved press list, and I clearly wasn't an employee, as my badge indicated. So, I was escorted out of the room. Never one to be deterred, however, I borrowed someone *else's* badge—a press pass, this time. I snuck back in, but it was only moments before security found me again.

"Justine, we told you, you're not allowed in here."

"Huh, you were serious about that?" I said, gesturing to my new pass. "I thought that was . . . you know . . . a joke? Or I just needed a different type of credential?"

It was not a joke. I was kicked out again. And it occurred to me that I might really be on Apple's blacklist. They did not want me in there. And they definitely didn't want me anywhere near Steve Jobs.

The thing was, I understood—by then I had my own fans. I'd hit a million Twitter followers, I was approaching half a million subscribers on YouTube, and that had given me a tiny taste of what it might be like to be really, *actually* famous. While the vast majority of folks who had friended or followed me online were sweet, lovely, normal people, I'd definitely come across the occasional weirdo, the kind of creep I would run away from if we ever so much as met in person. So, I mean, *iJustine*? Assuming Jobs actually did know who I was (and I'm fairly certain he was at least *aware* of my existence, seeing as how he ran away from me at our last almost-meeting), I can't blame him for steering clear. I always assumed it was fairly obvious that I was playing up the "obsession" angle for the camera, but it has occurred to me over the years that maybe I should've been a little less, well, *crazy*.

. . .

The next few years passed by in a blur—I hit 1 million subscribers on YouTube, and I got the chance to do some more on-camera television work, including a stint on *Criminal Minds* (I died again, this time after being chased through a cornfield by a couple of psychopaths in a pickup truck), as well as a recurring gig working as a correspondent for GTECH and Spike TV. I was doing well enough that I was even able to do some "work" on occasion with my sisters, too.

My sisters have always had a kind of front-row seat to my weird, crazy life online—since they've essentially grown up with it, I think

they've more or less gotten used to having a camera around. For example, Breanne—who is a pharmacist now—is no longer surprised when a customer asks for a selfie with his flu shot. As for Jenna, we've always had a bit more in common (we both love video games and fooling around online—Breanne, on the other hand, is the least tech savvy of the three of us), so it was only natural that she'd end up in an increasing number of my videos over the years. Eventually, I started badgering her to create her own YouTube channel, and despite being really hesitant at first, she quickly found that she enjoyed the online world. Since moving to L.A., she's discovered she's good at it, too. She works for a public relations firm, focusing on social media initiatives, and based on her unique background, she has a perspective almost no one else in the field has—she intuitively understands what will work online, what won't, and why. We have a few joint projects in the pipeline, and I'm excited to see what we'll come up with next.

In 2011, the three of us got together to found Squatch Watch, southwestern Pennsylvania's resident Sasquatch-hunting team (a spoof, obviously, on Animal Planet's *Finding Bigfoot*)—which has since

ballooned to four whole members: me; Jenna (our night vision coordinator, who once rigged a GoPro to the dashboard of our vehicle with nothing but Band-Aids); Breanne (who adamantly refused to be on camera until I dragged her into the frame); and Steve, our safety and explosives expert, in whose honor I made that first website so many years ago.

Dez and I also continued to make videos sporadically—including the time I made her sneak me into an elevator in her office building because Heinz had some kind of corporate outpost there (I have a weird obsession with ketchup)—but 2011 was a big year for her, too, for a different reason: she got engaged. (I enjoyed her off-line wedding, and did not shoot or post any weird videos from her big day.)

• • •

In October of that year, I was having lunch with a friend when my phone started pinging and vibrating, signaling a slew of incoming texts: "I'm sorry," they said. "I know how much he meant to you," they said. "Are you okay?" I immediately got that awful, sinking feeling in my gut, that moment when you know something terrible has happened, but you don't yet know what it is. I navigated over to Twitter; my entire feed was filled with condolences. And that's when I realized what had happened. Steve Jobs had died.

Right there in the middle of a diner, I cried.

You might think deciding to film my reaction was an odd choice, but I knew it was something my followers would expect; Steve Jobs had been too monumentally influential in my life to ignore his passing. Still, I disabled the embedded advertisements (so I wouldn't make any kind of commission based on views), I posted it without any obvious tags, without using his name in the video's title, and I buried it in "iJustine's iPhone," the least subscribed to of all my You-Tube channels. I was naive enough to think that only those who followed me closely would find it; by posting the video, I had hoped that, in some small way, we could grieve together. That, of course, is exactly the opposite of what happened: the video ended up on the front page of Reddit within twenty-four hours. Overnight, I was approaching a million views.

The backlash was swift and ferocious: I was exploiting his death; I was faking my sadness. I was also wearing leather boots in the video, which at some point rubbed together underneath the table I was sitting at, creating a rather unfortunate sound, which became a rather unfortunate headline: "iJustine Farts After Death of Steve Jobs." If I hadn't been so depressed at the time, it would've been funny, I guess.

I never got a chance to meet Steve Jobs. I have no idea what he would think of the work that I do, or my "obsession" with him, or the fact that my name is an homage to one of his products. Sometimes I'm almost glad we didn't meet. By all accounts, he could be arrogant and difficult and unyielding; he could be petulant, abrasive, and even mean. It's possible—likely, even—that the myth I had built up in my head wouldn't match the man. And yet he—perhaps more than anyone else in my life—was the one who inspired me to embrace the weird, silly, unique things about myself that make me *me*.

And that's why Steve Jobs was so much more than an inventor of sleek gadgets or a powerful businessman; he was someone who inspired awe, who made us marvel, who made people believe that anything was possible. He was a genius who wasn't afraid to think differently, and I miss him.

FAIR GAME

WHEN I WAS A KID, MY FAMILY AND I SPENT VIRTUALLY EVERY CHRISTMAS EVE OVER AT MY FRIEND CJ'S HOUSE. His mother used to throw these wonderfully elaborate holiday parties—decorations everywhere, music playing. But what I remember most about those nights isn't singing Christmas carols or trimming the tree; it's sitting in front of the television with CJ and his brothers, waiting patiently (sometimes not so patiently) for my turn to play Mortal Kombat II. We weren't allowed to have the Mortal Kombat games at my house; my mother thought they were too violent.

Like a lot of eighties babies, I can chart the course of my childhood less by the year than by the video games I was playing: huge swaths of early elementary school were spent with my butt in that too-small rocking chair, eating Nintendo snacks, playing the original Super Mario Bros. Shortly before transitioning out of middle school, I'd discovered The 7th Guest on CD-ROM, a game so creepy—it was set in a haunted mansion— that just thinking about it now is enough to give me the chills.* And by

---

*I actually just downloaded The 7th Guest from the Internet so I could play it again for the first time in years. Verdict: amazingly nostalgic. Also, still creepy.

high school I had entered the world of PC gaming (even though I didn't have a PC at the time), playing Quake and Unreal Tournament at LAN parties with members of the 1337 Crew.

As I got older I continued to play games casually, and at one point or another I owned many of the most popular consoles. (You'll remember, for example, that I camped out at Walmart for the launch of the PlayStation 3.) Whatever equipment I had amassed, however, stayed behind in Pittsburgh when I eventually made the move to California, and for a time, I played less often than I once did. For a brief period in my early twenties, I was far more consumed by trying to make a living than gaming.

It was in that rocky in-between, when I was still living at my manager's house and spending an increasing amount of time with Brookers, that I had my first introduction to World of Warcraft. One of our friends was a huge fan at the time, and it had already become such an iconic game that I figured I'd go ahead and sign up for my free trial. Of course, I had no idea how to play—I was playing on a Mac laptop, no less—and after realizing I had to slice a "rabbit" in half (which was actually a boar), I was suddenly overcome with giddy laughter, the kind of contagious cackling where you just can't quite catch your breath, the kind of wonderful silliness that sometimes occurs, out of thin air, when you're hanging out with one of your closest friends. Brooke was there to film the whole thing, and she deemed my over-the-top shrieking "the best n00b reaction ever," which became the title of the video that I promptly posted to YouTube.

That video has since been viewed nearly a million times, and let's just say the reaction has been, uh, *mixed*. Some people seemed to genuinely enjoy my enthusiasm, others suggested that I was faking it for the camera, and, of course, there were plenty of those ever-charming references to a woman's place being in the kitchen. I've never been asked to make a sandwich so many times in my life. There were also lots of accusations that I wasn't a "real" gamer or that I was pretending to like WoW, which I never quite understood, since the video made it quite clear that I had never played before. Finally, I received a host of emails yelling at me for using the arrow keys rather than WASD (and if you have to ask what that means, well, I would caution you about posting your own WoW video to the Internet).

Behind the scenes, however, those first few moments of sheer silliness had turned into hours and hours of game play—I quickly graduated from playing in my spare time to playing even when I didn't have any time to waste. Gaming, of course, will do that to you; it's addictive. Instead of going out on the weekends, I'd snuggle up on the couch, chatting with my sister on Xbox Live. Sometimes my mom would take the headset to chat a little, too. Gaming, for me, was (and is!) a relaxing escape from reality.

By 2011 I had more stability than I had ever had in my adult life. I actually had some disposable income, too, most of which was spent on computer upgrades, cameras, and gaming equipment. The increasing amount of time I spent playing games, however, was time that I wasn't devoting to making videos and posting them to the web. As I've said before, my business isn't self-sustaining; it relies on a near constant output of content. For that reason, it made sense—to me, at least—to start a gaming channel.

That got me a fair amount of flak, too. I certainly wasn't the first person to start a YouTube channel devoted solely to gaming; several of my friends, in fact, were already managing their own. That same year,

Justin Kan had transitioned Justin.tv to Twitch.tv, an entire platform devoted to not just gaming videos but game live-streaming. To people with only a casual notion of who I was, the move was seen as a play for money; it seemed like my "sudden" interest in video games had been invented for the sole purpose of cashing in on a newly popular phenomenon. There wasn't enough "evidence" out there of my previous gaming experience to convince some people that I wasn't full of it.

But that bit of backlash was nothing compared to the heat I got after posting my first Let's Play.

1 year ago
What is the most embarrassing thing you've ever done on video?

Let's Play videos, to the supremely uninitiated, are video game playthroughs with voice-over commentary. There are all kinds of reasons to watch—to get a sense if a particular game is worth buying; to enjoy a particular gamer's brand of commentary (some gamers discuss skill and strategy while others focus more on being quirky or comedic for entertainment's sake); or just for the pleasure of spectating (after all, we watch other people play all kinds of sports; we even watch other people *cook* for entertainment—why not watch them play video games?). I realize now, though, that I didn't know *enough* about the culture I was getting ready to insert myself into. For my first Let's Play, I chose a game I had never played before—one I knew nothing about, in fact—in a genre that wasn't even my forte (I prefer first-person shooter, or FPS, games). That game was Portal 2. And I wasn't just bad; I might be the worst Portal 2 player that's ever lived. And if you think I'm exaggerating, just ask the Internet.

I got absolutely slaughtered. Once the hard-core gamers got hold of it, the vitriol exploded: I was the stupidest person ever. I was giving girl gamers a bad name. I should die. I should kill myself. I should be "blasted off into space along with the rest of such idiots" (and, yes, that's an actual comment). I finished the game—in an admittedly long, tedious series of videos, which I later made private after receiving a rush of increasingly intense, violent, and graphic death threats. (There have been a few times that I've experienced a wave of particularly hateful comments online; this was one of them.)

Making the videos private wasn't enough, though, because the legacy of my awful Portal 2 playing has followed me. YouTube is littered with mirrors of the original videos, many of which feature new, considerably less flattering commentary. A Reddit "Ask Me Anything" I participated in several years ago took a nasty turn when Portal came up, and eventually it dominated the thread. (Things got heated and ugly enough that some Redditors actually felt the need to apologize for the general tenor of the conversation, if you can believe it.)

In 2014 I was asked to present at the Game Awards in Las Vegas— the ceremony is streamed live across several different gaming and video platforms, including Xbox, PlayStation, Twitch, and YouTube. Immediately afterward, I hopped on a plane to San Jose to attend a League of Legends event hosted by Intel Extreme Masters (IEM), which is an international e-sports tournament series that culminates each year in a World Championship. The Internet lit up again; apparently there was enough outrage about my appearance at the Game Awards that I briefly became a trending topic on Twitter.

. . .

It would be really, really easy—too easy, in fact—to write off comments like these as the work of haters, trolls, or just inherently mean and nasty people, but I think the truth is probably a bit more complicated. Gaming, after all, is still a relatively young culture; modern gaming as we know it has been around for only thirty-some-odd years, and for much of that time, being a "gamer" was associated with social marginalization. Gamers, not unlike hackers or geeks, were portrayed as nerdy outcasts and misfits. Gaming was (wrongfully) considered the domain of awkward adolescent boys with no social skills. That view is still so pervasive that most depictions of gamers in mainstream and pop culture are of friendless, wife- or girlfriend-less losers. Steve Carell plays the ultimate version of this stereotype in *The 40-Year-Old Virgin*; not only does his character play video games and collect action figures, but the fact that he owns an elaborate video game chair, complete with surround-sound speakers and joysticks mounted to the armrests, is used to signal just how much of a loser he really is. (But seriously, where can I get one of those, because it is *awesome*?) In the cult film *Grandma's Boy,* the main character, a video game tester, is forced to move in with his grandmother after being evicted from his apartment; his best friend and coworker is a grown man who lives with his parents, sucks his thumb at night, and sleeps in a child's car bed. But the same way that, say, members of the 1337 Crew took pride in our "otherness"—by making T-shirts, by thinking of ourselves as both skilled and *elite,* by turning something nerdy into something cool—

many in the gaming community have embraced their membership in what was, for a long time, an exclusive club; being a gamer was special, in part, because it *wasn't* mainstream. It's only relatively recently that our ideas about gaming culture, about what makes a "true" gamer, have started to change.

Although still heavily associated with teenage boys, the majority of gamers are actually adults, a growing percentage of which are women. Some studies put that number at just under 50 percent (although it's worth pointing out that those studies use an admittedly broad definition of gaming, including those played on mobile devices—and I think most serious gamers wouldn't consider Candy Crush a part of their culture). But as the gaming industry has grown—both conceptually as well as in size—it has also fractured: it's now possible to classify gamers as either casual, core, or hard-core, even though none of those terms have agreed-upon, universal definitions. What we're seeing as a result of all this change, I think, is a kind of internal culture war.

Gamergate is the most obvious and recent example of that war, and it has snowballed to encompass a wide array of seemingly unrelated issues, from accusations of corruption in video game journalism to alleged collusion between video game developers and reviewers to widespread concerns about misogyny in the industry. What's made Gamergate so explosive, in fact, have been the allegations of harassment and abuse directed at a small group of women in the gaming world. Since I'm neither a developer, a professional reviewer, or a gaming journalist, I'll leave the political discussions to other people—nor do I want to weigh in on what should or should not be represented in video games themselves; some of *my* favorite games, including Call of

Duty and Grand Theft Auto, are often the most maligned by the mainstream press, anyway. But I do think it's pretty clear that a small yet vocal contingent feels the gaming community has been hijacked by "outsiders." There's a battle for authenticity raging; hence the accusations about who is and who isn't a "real" gamer, who loves gaming for its own sake, and who's just faking it—for attention, to be cool (because in some circles, gaming is cool now), or to cash in.

Interestingly, this same debate is also popping up in the larger world of YouTube. As the site has grown, it too has fractured: small content creators (who work alone, with no funding—exactly the place I started from) are often pitted against the "big YouTubers," people (like me, now) who run partner channels, who might produce sponsored videos on occasion, and who generally pull in large numbers of views. Big YouTubers are sometimes seen as inauthentic simply because of their popularity; the more views we receive, or the more we may branch out into new genres of content, or the more YouTube itself publicizes, promotes, and supports its largest contributors, the more likely we are to be accused of having sold out.

What's unfortunate about debates like these—aside from the fact that they're just flat-out unwinnable—is that while each side hurls insults at the other (in the wake of Gamergate, for example, we're seeing the word *gamer* being used as a pejorative all over again; we're right back to suggesting that anyone who likes video games must be a misogynistic, lunkheaded caveman), some truly awful behavior is being normalized. I worry about how easily things escalate from an anonymous comment posted in a chat room or in response to a video, to a more personal attack directed at someone's Twitter feed or private email account, to more extreme activities, like harassment, hacking, and doxxing. I can't tell you how many times I've read comments online—about myself and about other people—wherein the author writes a variation of the following:

"I'm just joking."

"I doubt she'll ever see this, anyway."

"She doesn't care about her viewers; she's only doing this for money."

"I don't *actually* mean I want her to die."

"I don't *actually* hate her."

"It's harmless."

And for the most part, it probably *is* harmless—all of us gossip, and I know that the vast majority of people who make lewd or even vaguely threatening statements online do not *actually* wish harm on the subject of those comments. But it is a slippery slope. And unfortunately I've seen firsthand what it's like when that line gets crossed.

It happened about a year ago. It was late—after midnight—and I was headed to bed with my then boyfriend when his cell phone started to ring. We tried ignoring it at first, but when we realized the caller wasn't going away, he answered. It was a representative from our home security company; the guy on the phone asked to speak with me. "That's weird," my boyfriend said, a concerned look on his face. He handed me the phone.

"Hello?" I said, sitting up a little in bed.

"Ma'am, I need you to hang up and call the police department immediately."

"What?" I shouted. "What's going on?!"

"Just hang up and call the police. You need to call them *right now*."

I didn't have a clue what the problem was, but I wasn't about to wait around to find out. I hung up and called the police; after living a relatively public life for so many years—after seeing what can happen—I have them on speed dial. I explained to the woman who answered that I had been instructed to call, but that I didn't know why. I wasn't sure if there was some kind of emergency, or was something wrong? But as soon as I gave her my address, she flew into crisis mode: "Is everything okay? Do you need an ambulance? Are you hurt?" she asked, the questions flying out of her mouth, rapid-fire.

"No?" I said, still confused. "I'm fine. I was sleeping. What exactly is going on?"

"Is there anyone else in the house with you?" she asked.

"Yes, my boyfriend is here. What is going on?" I repeated.

"Is *he* okay? Does he have any weapons or anything?"

"*What?*" I said again. "No! *He's* fine. He's sleeping. What. Is. Going. On?" I asked for a third time.

The woman was not interested in my questions. "I need you both to walk outside with your hands up, okay? There will be officers there to greet you."

She actually said "greet you," by the way—I remember that very clearly—as if we were going to have some kind of friendly get-together with the members of the police department in the front lawn of my apartment building. At that point, my heart was thumping out of my chest and I kept casting suspicious looks at my boyfriend, like, did *you* do something? *What in the hell did you do?*

We walked outside with our hands up, as instructed—though, of course, I was on the phone the entire time—straight into the arms of five police officers poised outside our home, guns drawn. I looked to the left, then to the right—the entire street had been shut down, barricaded at either end. Just as I'd finished counting the number of black-and-white patrol cars lining the block (ten), a group of officers ran by, straight into the house. My boyfriend and I were each patted down and searched for weapons. Once the cops were able to determine that the scene was safe, that there was no emergency, they finally told us what had happened: an anonymous caller claimed that my boyfriend (whose name the caller knew, almost certainly because of his online presence) had killed me, was about to kill our children (despite the fact that, of course, we didn't have kids), and there was a bomb inside our home. We'd been swatted.

We were lucky, for many reasons: that the incident was over before any news media could arrive on the scene; that the cops, who had been suspicious about the call from the start, didn't feel the need to break our door down (when they tried to return the original call and couldn't get through, they figured—correctly, as it turns out—that the "emergency" was likely a prank; rather than break our door down, they kept trying to reach *us* on the telephone instead); that—in a moment when adrenaline is pumping, weapons are drawn, and confusion abounds—no one was hurt. But as I looked around my neighborhood, I saw how many people had been affected, far more than just my boyfriend and me. Snipers were positioned on the roofs of the adjacent buildings; the cops would have had to gain entry to countless homes, waking people up in the middle of the night, telling them God knows what. Obviously, prank calls like these are a massive drain on public resources, as well as wildly expensive—as much as ten thousand dollars per incident. I can only hope that no other *actual* emergency was occurring somewhere in the vicinity at the same time, the victims of which would have been endangered by the fact that half the police department had been called to my house, for nothing. I've known people, however, who weren't so lucky: the same thing happened to someone else I know, only the raid was considerably more violent; someone in that house was knocked so forcefully to the ground (because he was briefly mistaken for an intruder) that he had to be hospitalized for a fairly serious concussion.

Swatting, of course, is not a new phenomenon, but it has spread into the gaming world—our experience was linked to a rash of prank calls associated with members of a particular gaming community. I want to point out that this had nothing to do with Gamergate, and it is in no way indicative of the broader gaming culture—these are individuals who are willfully and purposefully breaking the law—and when the people perpetrating this kind of behavior call themselves gamers, we all lose.

Look, I was posting videos on YouTube within six months of the site's launch. I joined Twitter before most people knew it existed. I was the 103rd person to sign up for an Instagram account (out of 300 million monthly active users). But you don't see me screaming at everyone to get off social media, threatening people because they're not "real" content creators, accusing people of using Twitter only because it's popular now, or suggesting that people who join Instagram this late in the game are only doing it to get attention. Furthermore, I *want* people to use these platforms, to learn about and enjoy new media, for no other reason than that I love tech. Likewise, I would never suggest that I am any more or less of an authentic gamer than somebody else. I may not identify as a professional gamer, but I love gaming all the same. I welcome anyone into the fold who wants to love it, too. I want *more* people to play games, not less. It doesn't have to be an "us" versus "them" kind of argument: there is not a limited supply of video games or Twitter accounts or YouTube channels in the world. What we say to each other—even when it's anonymous, even when we think no one is paying attention, even when it's *online*—matters. Words have meaning. I'd rather us all win.

. . .

Speaking of welcoming anyone into the fold, my grandmother Grayce—the same woman who used to watch *TechTV* with me in the afternoon after school—has jumped on board with just about everything I've been doing. We got her set up with her first computer (a green iMac) years ago, hooked her up to Facebook, signed her up for Twitter, and unleashed her on the Internet. Any time a new social network comes out, she is *on* it. Although she still wasn't a *gamer* (unless you count, like, sudoku as gaming), she did once march into a local GameStop and try to buy an Xbox because she wanted to watch the Call of Duty event I was hosting. I tried to explain that she could just stream the show online, but she definitely went in there and started telling all the employees that they had to watch the upcoming Call of Duty Championships because her granddaughter would be on it. Not long after that, I just gave her one of my old Xbox consoles. Sure enough, the next time my sister Jenna went over for a visit, she found our grandmother playing the game I had left inside, Call of Duty: Black Ops. *My grandmother was playing Black Ops.* Jenna dutifully sent me some Snapchat proof, and I knew my work there was done.

• • •

I had no idea the ways in which video games would have a profound effect on my life—beyond just the enjoyment of playing them—but I have gotten to know so many people in the gaming community, on the developer side, in the competitive and professional worlds, and just regular people I meet at events and tournaments and online, and they are some of the most creative, passionate, and enthusiastic people I know. I've gotten the chance to work with the Call of Duty team and Activision Publishing a lot in particular, hosting a number of events, even shooting a small role in the Call of Duty: Black Ops 2 live-action trailer. It's pretty incredible when video games have so influenced popular culture that award-winning directors like Guy Ritchie and actors like Robert Downey Jr. want to participate in these kinds of projects. The trailer, by the way, features a chain of "players" sneaking up behind one another and yelling "Surprise!" before trying to take out their respective targets. I spent a day on set—pretending to throw a combat axe in some guy's back—but my actual line of dialogue was recorded in-studio, in a process called ADR, or "automated dialogue replacement." You're supposed to say the line lots of different ways, using lots of different inflections, so that the director can choose the most appropriate delivery. I swear I said "surprise" fifty different times—I said it joyfully, seriously, menacingly, quietly, loudly, in a whisper, in a shout. Finally I had to be like, guys? I'm out of ways to say this one word. I got nothing else.

We have come such a long way from those old-school graphics and boxy controllers that so many of us grew up with. Remembering what it felt like to sit in that too-small rocking chair, chomping on Nintendo snacks, gives me an even greater appreciation for the incredible technology, artistry, and storytelling that goes into modern video games. But the originals will always have a special place in my heart. So you can imagine my response when I received an email from someone at Nintendo asking if I wanted to interview Shigeru Miyamoto—general manager at Nintendo Entertainment Analysis & Development and creator of some of the most iconic and beloved video game characters in history, including Mario, Donkey Kong, Zelda, and Star Fox—to discuss the impending release of Mario Maker and the upcoming thirtieth anniversary of Super Mario Bros. One of the hardest things I've ever done is to try and play it cool on the phone when I called the woman back—"Uh-huh . . . uh-huh . . . yes, that sounds fine . . . yes, I think I'm free." Meanwhile I was running around behind the scenes like, "Clear my schedule! CANCEL *EVERYTHING*!" I couldn't believe this was real life. I actually cried.

We shot several videos, one of which was just a straight interview. The others featured me, Mr. Miyamoto, and Bill Trinen, senior product marketing manager at Nintendo, playing Mario Kart 8—which was surreal, and also kind of high-pressure; I have poor eyesight even with glasses or contacts and the television was positioned on the far side of the room. Between being nervous and excited and pretty much blind, I didn't exactly put in my best performance. Meeting him, though, was a dream come true. It would be hard to find a child born within the last thirty-plus years whose life that man hasn't touched. And if that doesn't say something about the power of video games on our lives, I don't know what to tell you.

ALMOST FAMOUS

I WAS STANDING ON THE RED CARPET AT THE MTV MOVIE AWARDS, CAMERA IN HAND. It was my first big Hollywood gig, and it was 2009—the year *Twilight* hit theaters—so there was a particular kind of frenzied excitement in the air; Robert Pattinson, Kristen Stewart, and Taylor Lautner, all of whom had just catapulted to mega-stardom, would be in attendance. So would the cast of *Harry Potter,* on hand to share an exclusive sneak peek of the next film in their wildly popular franchise. Pretty much every major star in the business, in fact, was due to show up, and reporters from all the big press outlets had been setting up cameras and mics for hours. Rickety metal bleachers—spectator stands—which had been erected for the sole purpose of stargazing, were now filled to capacity with picture-taking, sign-wielding, screaming teenage fans. From my position near the end of the press line, twenty or so feet from the venue's stage door, I could just make out the first few celebrity arrivals. I watched as a steady stream of famous musicians and movie stars exited their vehicles, waved to the crowd, and began making their way along the carpet, drawing closer and closer to me with each step. And that's when I realized I had a problem.

I didn't have the slightest idea who any of these people were.

I mean, sure, I could pick, like, Denzel Washington or Will Ferrell out of a lineup, but the girls from *The Hills*? The cast of *Gossip Girl*? No way. I'd just never been all that up on the Hollywood scene, and other than watching *TechTV* in the afternoons, I didn't spend much time in front of the tube growing up. To me, people like Leo Laporte and Alex Lindsay and Steve Jobs were celebrities. So, as I stood on the carpet with a rep from the company that had invited me to cover this event, I surreptitiously pointed at some of the most famous people in the world and confessed, "I don't know who he is. I don't know who she is. I don't know who that guy is, either." I thought three MTV interns were the Jonas Brothers.

Luckily, I had a group of giddy young girls to help me—they'd positioned themselves behind me (incidentally, behind a thick row of hedges, too), hoping to get a better view of the stars right before they ducked inside the theater. Every time someone I didn't recognize approached (which was pretty often), I'd look over my shoulder and shrug, and they'd scream out, "That's the dad from *Twilight*!" or "That's the guy from *Transformers*!" At some point, after I got tired of shouting out a bunch of names in the hopes of scoring an interview—"Peter!!! Tyrese!!"—I just started yelling "Yay" at people. I literally just screamed "Yay!!" at Ed Helms from *The Office*. It was awkward.

I've learned a lot since then, of course—I mean, these days I'm sort of supposed to know what's up and who's who. But the fact that I started out *not* knowing means that I never thought celebrities were inherently cool. I've gotten more and more opportunities to speak with actors and musicians and comedians over the years—either on the red carpet, on behalf of shows like *Entertainment Tonight* or *E! News*, or just for my own YouTube channel—but it's never been someone's fame that I've found impressive or inspiring. As I learned way back in my American Eagle days, I just like talking to people. I don't care if you starred in the biggest summer blockbuster or you're my next-door neighbor; any opportunity to have a great conversation is pretty amazing. Which is why when it comes to celebrity interviews, it's the quality of the conversation I care most about. I try to ask somewhat unique or unexpected questions, and whenever I get the chance to have some fun, I usually do. These days my interview style is much more "what's your favorite video game?" than "who are you wearing?"

When I sat down with Vince Vaughn during the press junket for his film *The Internship,* for example, we played a quick game of Operation. Rather than talk about his musical inspiration, I asked Jack Johnson if he'd make a funny GIF with me before his performance at the Hangout Music Festival. I also have a long—admittedly weird—history of asking people what their favorite treat is. (I don't really know what to tell you

Vince Vaughn is explaining to me why he thinks kids are better than adults at Operation: Little Hands. (Personally, I think he was just trying to set the bar low . . .)

about that; I like treats, okay? My first blog was called tastyblogsnack. My podcast with Dez was *Mommy Pack My Lunch*. You'd think I didn't get fed as a child!) Most people need a minute or two to register what I mean by *treat*—I typically have to specify that I mean *food*—but then they happily comply: Jay Leno likes a root beer float. Jack Black likes quesadillas stuffed with Doritos. Ashton Kutcher likes a "coconut caramel graham cracker thing" he once had in Puerto Vallarta. Jeff Bezos, CEO of Amazon, likes bread pudding. Billy Bob Thornton likes German chocolate cake.

Of course, I don't always have the freedom to ask whatever I want. I'm not always able to bring a board game to a press junket or to shove a microphone in someone's face and inquire about his or her favorite treat—the Oscars red carpet, for example, tends to be a pretty buttoned-up affair. In fact, at some events you'll be supplied with a list of questions from which you really are not supposed to deviate. That's why I prefer doing interviews for a more relaxed, web-based audience; I'd rather cover an event where it's okay to be my regular goofy self, where I won't get my hand slapped if I choose not to ask a certain famous woman about her new book of selfies or her diet regimen.

And speaking of my regular goofy self, the most memorable Hollywood moment of my career occurred at the 2014 Academy Awards, for completely nonglamorous, noncelebrity-related reasons. I was covering the red carpet for the Associated Press and Banana Republic, and I only had one real goal in mind for the evening. I'd just seen one of the most amazing films in cinematic history, and though this masterpiece wouldn't be eligible for an Oscar nomination until the following year, I was so moved by it that I wanted to make some kind of grand public gesture.

Obviously, I am talking about *The LEGO Movie*.

Like every other eighties kid in America, I've loved LEGO since childhood. I love them so much, however, that after seeing the movie I went to eBay and started purchasing every character—even the characters that had only a one- or two-second cameo, I wanted. Now I was at the Oscars with a purse full of LEGO figures and a dream. The carpet was already teeming with publicists, cameramen, and reporters. It was also a soggy mess, since it had been raining in L.A. for two days straight. But I would not be deterred. I would do whatever I had to do to *get the shot*. I plopped right down in the middle of it all, I just lay down right there in the middle of the red carpet, strategically placed the LEGO figures side by side, arranging them as if they'd just stepped out of their limo, snapped a few photos, and suddenly felt my entire body being lifted into the air by a couple of (very strong) security guards.

I'm not sure who was more embarrassed: them, for having to pick someone up off the floor at one of the most prestigious industry events of the year, or me . . . for that exact same reason.

• • •

As is perhaps becoming obvious, I don't put a lot of stock in the notion of celebrity. I'm not easily swayed by the goings-on in Hollywood. But over the years, I've started to get a growing number of messages, tweets, and comments like this:

@ijustine I really wanna be famous like you and have a really cool webcast as you. How did you get started? can you help me get noticed?

3:17 PM - 29 Aug 2010

And that feels weird. It was never my goal to get famous. (If it *had* been my goal, certainly there would have been better ways to go about it than posting videos of me dancing awkwardly or getting fruit lobbed at my head.) My goal—if you could even call it that, back when I was first starting out—was to somehow earn enough money to survive while pursuing the things I most loved: technology, gadgets, and gaming. I knew I wanted to work for myself—after my awful experience at the chiropractor's office, I valued that more than ever—doing something I truly enjoyed. Beyond that, though, I was pretty much winging it. There was no master plan. Fame, Internet or otherwise, was an unlikely, unexpected by-product.

The thing about YouTube is that it feels so *immediate*—the content tends to be stripped down and raw (the total opposite of a slick Hollywood production); the majority of videos are shot with basic, readily available, inexpensive equipment, not on the floor of some set or studio, but in someone's regular old living room or bedroom. (Remember, my first green screen was a cheap blanket from IKEA.) As for the content creators themselves, they're not delivering perfectly polished sound bites via an A-list publicist; they're speaking frankly, straight to the camera, about relatable, everyday topics, engaging directly with their followers and fans. Whereas just about everything that comes out of Hollywood feels manufactured, the content on YouTube feels authentic and more accessible. It really shouldn't be surprising that YouTube stars are now more recognizable and influential to teenage audiences than Hollywood stars.

The savviest mainstream celebrities not only recognize this, they're incorporating that knowledge back into their highly stylized public images. Near the end of 2014, for example, Beyoncé released a (totally awesome) music video for her song "7/11" that was shot on a couple of GoPros. She's one of the wealthiest and most successful entertainers in the world—there's a reason they call her the Queen—but the video was *intended* to look grainy and homemade. It feels so spontaneous and voyeuristic, in fact—like you've been granted a rare glimpse into her private life—that it's easy to forget you're watching a highly choreographed and expertly edited production. (As a video editor, I can tell you that the finished product is anything but amateur.) It's easy to forget that she's not showing us anything she doesn't *want* us to see.

Likewise, it's easy to forget that the average YouTube video isn't "real," either—just like any other kind of content, YouTube clips are planned, filmed (often in multiple takes), edited (mistakes and bloopers can be cut out), and in many (if not most) instances, semi-scripted. That doesn't mean they are, in fact, inauthentic—I genuinely think that most YouTubers believe what they say on camera; I certainly don't just make things up when I'm shooting a video—but they aren't an accurate and full depiction of any one person's life.

Sometime in the years between 2009 and 2011, I made the transition from just trying to make enough money to survive to running an actual business. It wasn't like I woke up one morning and had a lot of money in the bank, or suddenly had a lot of people working for me—there wasn't a specific day or week when it happened; I couldn't pinpoint a moment when things shifted if I tried. But the thing I had been creating for so many years had grown enough that I had real responsibilities. And part of running a successful business—maybe the first step—is knowing your audience.

The bulk of *my* audience is preteen and teenage girls (which is to be expected—almost all YouTube content creators have very young audiences; after all, young people are the most active on social media, and they also consume way more digital content than adults). Over time I have adjusted my content accordingly: I rarely curse on camera; I don't drink on camera, either; nor do I work with alcohol companies—even though I've been offered enormous sums of money to do so. I don't talk about boyfriends, family drama, work issues, or fights with my friends, because I don't think that's anyone's business. None of these things mean I'm creating inauthentic content, but rather that I'm creating content with my audience in mind (as well as keeping at least a sliver of my life to myself).

The same way that what you see on camera is not a full depiction of any one person's life, it's also not a true depiction of what it's like to live in the public eye. No one who's making regular content for YouTube (or any other platform) is showing you something they don't want you to see. I often tell people they can't believe everything they read (or, increasingly, everything they watch), but it's difficult to explain why without telling the whole story, and some things just aren't meant for public consumption. (Sorry.) What I will say is that based on my (very scientific) calculations, at *least* 50 percent of what gets said in the press and online is complete and total BS. I have a running joke with some of my friends about when we're going to schedule our wardrobe malfunctions—"Just so you know, I'm going to be having a nip slip on October 25! Make sure and tune in!"—a nod to the fact that so much of what seems accidental or spontaneous (paparazzi photos, public spats, budding romances) is often planned, usually by a team of professionals, well in advance.

Even when you know this, by the way, it's still possible to forget that you know it. Several years ago, I was doing some correspondent work at another awards show. I was between interviews on the carpet, when one of the producers I was working with stepped behind me and whispered in my ear, "Oh, there's so-and-so!" As it dawned on me that I was going to have to actually speak with this person, I did my best to stifle an audible groan. I don't think this person is a particularly great role model, and I don't particularly want to be associated with her. But I wasn't working for myself that evening; I was reporting on behalf of a television outfit—it didn't really matter what I thought, in other words. My job was to get the interview.

It did not go well. I didn't have a clue what to ask. For the first time in a long time, I had to have the questions fed to me—we ended up talking about diet plans and clothing designers, two topics I frankly couldn't care less about. (To top it off, she actually had to check the label inside her dress because she didn't know who she was wearing—it took all my strength not to scream at her, "*Girl*, you have ONE JOB!") Just when I thought the torture had ended, my producer started pressuring me to get a selfie. The last thing I wanted was a photo with this woman, but I suffered through it, gritting my teeth the entire time.

It was only a day or so later, when I was editing the footage to post on YouTube, that a thought occurred to me: I had to admit that I didn't actually *know* this woman. My perception of her was based entirely on what's been written about her in the press, as well as what she posts to Instagram and Twitter and YouTube. I might not respect her public persona—and I deleted all evidence of our interview from the video I eventually posted online—but I had to remind myself that I knew absolutely nothing about her private life. For all I know, she's a perfectly wonderful person. Maybe everything I *thought* I knew about her wasn't actually true? I hate being judged—I hate being accused of things that I did not and would not do—and yet I had done much the same to her. Without even realizing it, I had been taking what the press said as gospel.

•　•　•

When I was first starting out, back in the Justin.tv days, what I loved most about living a life online was the people—it was easy enough to weed out the creeps and the crazies, as well as the folks who only wanted to use me to promote their own projects. (There's nothing worse than thinking you've made a new friend, only to have them say—a day or two after making your acquaintance—"By the way, could you tweet about this?") Everyone else, I was happy to follow online. Some of those people have followed me for years; some of them, I've followed for more than half their lives.

Kimberly and I met in the Justin.tv chat rooms—she was super active in those days, constantly commenting on the live feed, as well as the videos I posted to YouTube. We became Facebook friends, too, and I kept up with her life from afar. One day, totally out of the blue, she popped online to let me know she had taken a job with Nike, and she'd be in L.A., opening a new retail store. I couldn't not show up. We had never met in person, I didn't really, truly *know* her, but at the same time, I'd known of her for the better part of ten years.

Cherilyn started watching my videos when she was in either late middle school or early high school—what I remember most was just how *young* she looked in her profile photos. When we finally met in person for the first time, at a meet-up in Seattle, I almost fell off my chair. The girl staring back at me wasn't a girl; she was a twenty-one-year-old college student, old enough to grab a drink with me if she wanted. We hadn't just been following each other online, we had grown up together.

What's ironic is that as my social network has grown, it's gotten harder to forge authentic relationships. It's no longer feasible to write back to everyone who writes to me. There are so many social media platforms that it's virtually impossible to wade through them all; it's even trickier to try to determine someone's true intentions. Sometimes I actually long for the Justin.tv days. But every now and then I'll have a moment when it's possible to make a truly profound connection.

Not long ago, I was walking down the street in Australia—a country I had never been to before—when a young girl wearing an iJustine hoodie suddenly ran up to greet me. I couldn't believe it. Apparently, the girl's mother couldn't believe it, either. "Oh my God," the mother said when she saw me. "I am *so* glad we found you."

"Sorry?" I said, utterly confused.

"We've been looking for you for three days." She turned and looked at her daughter. "*Now* she can go home and study."

"She" was Alexandra, who knew—based on my Twitter feed—that I was in town, and had been walking the streets of Sydney, just hoping we might bump into each other. How magical is that? To touch someone who lives on the other side of the world, someone whom you've never met? To have a moment to talk about what she's studying in school or what she wants to do with her life? To run into someone who couldn't be happier to see you? To be able to follow her now, to watch her life unfold from 7,500 miles away? *That* is what's real. That is why I love what I do. That is the power of social media.

Alexandra 🐦
@AllyLandels

+⚫ **Follow**

@ijustine I can't believe I just met u!! My
dreams have come true 😍 😂

↩ 🔁 ★ •••

5:46 PM - 14 Feb 2015

• • •

There's a new study out that says the majority of teenagers like watching content on YouTube "because it makes them feel good"—so it's not so much about how they feel about the person they're watching but how the person they are watching makes them feel about themselves. That's why I've said (about 200 pages or so back, if you need a refresher) that what I do for a living is really not about *me*. That's why it worries me when I get messages from people who seemingly just want to be famous. It shouldn't be about getting famous. It shouldn't be about the size of your following. It should be about the way in which you connect with people in the world around you. It's about finding what you're truly passionate about, and letting that guide you. Fame is fleeting. But if you're really lucky, doing what you love can last forever.

MEANT TO BE

NOT TOO LONG AGO, MY MOTHER'S CELL PHONE WAS STOLEN. I completely freaked out at first because, for some unknowable reason, she had *refused* to put a passcode on the thing—despite repeated admonishing from all three of her daughters—but I pulled myself together long enough to help her remotely lock it and wipe the data. I was also able to track the phone to a nearby shipping facility—and I can't say I was all that surprised.

These days, smartphone theft has turned into a helluva business. Every year, millions of phones get swiped, wiped, and shipped out—often overseas—where they can be resold at huge profit margins. The FBI has been trying to crack down on this kind of activity for a while now; it's why kill switches were invented in the first place. In fact, in some states (namely California), kill switches are now required by law. So, as I said, I wasn't surprised that my mom's phone was already headed out of town. What I was surprised at was just how *fast* it all happened: someone had found the phone, swiped it, and most likely sold it to a fence or a middleman—who was now shipping the phone God knows where—inside of two or three hours.

I knew it wasn't likely we'd ever see the phone again, of course, but we stopped in to a local police station anyway, just to see if they might send an officer out to the shipping place, just to see if the phone was still there. The cop we ended up speaking with was a nice enough guy, an older fellow, but he wasn't exactly Sherlock Holmes, if you know what I mean. It was painfully clear this wasn't someone with a lot of experience, say, taking down criminal masterminds or busting international crime syndicates. As soon as I began explaining our situation, I could tell he just didn't get it.

"Well, that's too bad," he said, furrowing his brow, "but it's probably at a pawnshop by now. . . ."

I sort of squinted my eyes and cocked my head to the side. "Um, no . . . the phone is at this shipping place. It's obviously being shipped out somewhere so it can be repackaged and resold."

He was already shaking his head before I'd even finished my sentence. "Nope, that's just not how these things work," he said. "Things like this just don't move that quickly."

I could feel myself getting frustrated. "Sir, I'm telling you where the phone is, and it's not sitting at a pawnshop. It's probably *already* been sold, and now it's being shipped to a buyer somewhere."

"Ma'am, I've been on the force for twenty years and—"

"Well, I've been on the *Internet* for twenty years!" I yelled at him—or, at least, it's what I *would* have yelled at him, but I just really, really didn't want to be rude (and I'll admit, that was a struggle). But in that moment, I realized the sheer size of our disconnect. This guy was stuck in the past, woefully unaware of the effects of modern technology on the world around him. It was a stark reminder of just how much things have changed, and what happens when you don't keep up: you get left behind.

One of the things I love about having a young fan base is that they keep me connected and up-to-date on whatever's new: apps, memes, platforms, trends. And there will *always* be something new. The only thing that's certain in the tech world is that things will continue to evolve and change.

The way we consume content is wildly different than it was just ten years ago. Back when I posted my first video on YouTube, hardly anyone was watching content that had been made exclusively for the web. Television was king, and consumers had virtually no control over programming. The digital revolution has changed all that. TiVos and DVRs made it possible to watch what you wanted *when* you wanted; tablets and smartphones made it possible to watch what you wanted *where* you wanted. Platforms like YouTube and Viddler and Revver and Myspace and Facebook and Twitter made it possible for anyone to become a content creator. These days, people are watching less TV and more digital media; they're subscribing to cable less often, opting instead for digital services like Netflix and Hulu.

Nobody knows for sure where we're going or what's going to happen next, although it seems to me that we are moving in the direction of even faster speeds and more immediacy. Apps like Vine and Snapchat, which provide content that's digestible in ten or twenty seconds, sometimes even less than that, seem to be the wave of the future. My guess is that anything that slows down the consumption of content—either videos that take too long to load, or prerolls (the ads that precede online videos) that can't be immediately bypassed—will prove to be the downfall of companies or web platforms that can't or won't adapt.

1 year ago
iJustine, have you ever thought when you might stop broadcasting your life to the internet? If so, what might you do then?

As for me, I'm on the lookout for what's next in my career, too. Although people often ask me, "What's your plan?" or "What are your goals?" I never know how to answer those questions. After all, if someone would have told me five years ago that this would be my life, I would have thought they were crazy. Five years from now, who knows what might be possible? Sometimes, in fact, I think the beauty is in not knowing. For now I'm going to continue doing what I've always done—making videos, chasing the latest tech, and talking about the things I love online.

In March 2014, I headed down to Austin again, this time to host the Gaming Awards during the interactive portion of SXSW. At some point during the flight—during which I was sandwiched between my sister Jenna and Adam, a member of the Southwest Airlines social media team—I thought it might be fun to dance down the middle of the narrow aisle with Pharrell's "Happy" blasting over the speakers. Like, in front of everyone. At thirty-five thousand feet. So, I did. And let me tell you, it was both ridiculously fun and completely embarrassing. The video got picked up by *Good Morning America* (I'm pretty sure the story was just "crazy woman dances on airplane"—no mention of who I am or what I do for a living), and quickly went viral. Not surprisingly, the reactions were mixed—a thread on Reddit, for example, labeled the whole thing "cringe-worthy." But that's okay. I'm okay with that.

Later that same year, in September, came the launch of the iPhone 6. After covering I don't know how many product releases over the years, I was determined to be the first in line for this one. The phone was scheduled to go on sale at 8 a.m. on a Friday morning, so Jenna and I showed up outside the store around 8 a.m. on *Wednesday* morning, two full days early. And man, were we early—the second (technically third) person didn't show up for roughly six hours.

Since September in L.A. is still really hot, Jenna and I came prepared: we brought two child-sized pop-up play tents, styled to look like Volkswagen camper vans (in which we intended to sleep), some

Ed Palumbo, me, my sister Jenna, and Jeff Burke. First-in-line achievement unlocked!

blankets, some umbrellas (for shade), and all the requisite phone and video equipment. We'd chosen an Apple Store located on the Third Street Promenade in Santa Monica, a popular outdoor shopping and dining area, so the sidewalks were filled with shoppers, tourists, and street musicians, enough hustle and bustle to keep us from getting bored. But we needn't have worried—by that afternoon, we'd had a chance to meet and speak with Cody LaScala.

Cody, though I'd never met him before, is something of a Santa Monica celebrity, as well as a regular at the Third Street Promenade Apple Store. He's outgoing and funny and kind of a flirt. He also happens to have cerebral palsy, the result of nearly drowning as a baby. He gets around with the help of a wheelchair and had been using an iPad to aid his communication—that is, until someone stole the thing right out from under him. On the day we met, he was back to tapping out messages with his nose on an outdated iPhone.

"Are you coming back to get an iPhone 6 on Friday?" I asked him.

He shook his head. "Can't afford it."

As we waved good-bye to each other, I couldn't help but feel guilty. I didn't realize then that he'd be back in my life in a big way, and soon.

By Thursday morning, Jenna and I were starting to feel a little drained—sleeping on the street amid a small group of total strangers isn't exactly a recipe for a restful night. We watched as municipal workers trucked in metal barricades with which to designate the queue—the same ones used by cops for crowd control or to line the streets during a parade, and yes, we were so early to this thing that we arrived before even the barricades were put into place. It was already hot; the sun was relentless. But I was buoyed by meeting and chatting with other folks who had begun to show up—either because they, too, loved Apple products, or because they wanted to be part of the spectacle, or because they just wanted to say they'd done it, or maybe because they just really, really needed a new phone. Some of my friends swung by at various points to check in and say hello. I even saw a few people I'd met before at meet-ups and other events. As the crowd continued to grow, it became clear that the Apple Store employees had begun their preparations: first they carted massive cardboard boxes (no doubt filled with phones) from the storage area in back onto the main sales floor, then they hung huge black curtains to obscure the view through the plateglass windows. And before long, Cody was back, too.

He kept offering to bring Jenna and me some water or to buy us a meal; I was totally touched by his kindness and generosity. But when he overhead a comment I made about auctioning off my phone—I had already cut a deal with eBay to auction off my old phone, the one I was standing in line to replace, for charity—I got to hear a little more about his story.

As a child, Cody made nine separate trips to a unique rehabilitation clinic in Poland. The therapy was life-changing, but it was also (obviously) cost-prohibitive and travel-intensive, not to mention unavailable in the U.S. Which is why Cody's mother, Lynette, eventually decided to found the NAPA Center, an L.A.-based therapeutic facility that caters to children with neurological and developmental delays. Because the LaScalas just could not be any more amazing, the NAPA Center also has a charitable giving arm, the NAPA Center Kids Foundation, which provides grants to help families of children with special needs. It took me about five minutes to realize I was going to donate the proceeds from the sale of my iPhone to Cody and his mother's charity.

By Thursday night, the queue had exploded—hundreds and hundreds of people had shown up to join the party, and the line stretched all the way down and around the block. If you've never participated in one of these launch events before, it's kind of amazing how much of a sense of camaraderie you feel even just walking up and down the line—watching while people play cards or read the newspaper or commiserate about the heat or share tips on where to find the cleanest public restroom; suddenly, you start to feel like a little community; you start to feel close to your neighbors.

By Friday morning, though, I was wiped. I'd barely slept, Jenna had developed a mild case of heat exhaustion, and it was difficult to muster enthusiasm. In fact, at one point during filming (because, obviously, I filmed this whole thing), I asked the people around me—in an over-the-top sort of cheerleaderesque voice—if they were excited, and everyone just sort of let out an audible groan (and then of course we all laughed at the absurdity of the situation). But just after dawn, things picked up again. The news vans began to arrive, and the Apple employees started to show up; everyone in line kind of perked up a bit—that, or their morning coffee started to kick in. (Luckily—for everyone involved—there was a strategically placed Starbucks just down the street.) Soon enough, the black curtains in the windows came down, and the employees lined up right down the middle of the store, almost like a military-style arch of swords (just without the weapons, of course). Then the clapping and the cheering started—all of a sudden people were pushing toward the front to take pictures or video. And right there in the middle of it all was Cody, smiling, laughing, and—I kid you not—wearing a GoPro on his head. I suddenly had a flashback to the time I had waited in line for an iPhone for hours even though I had no hope of getting one; the phone I later received had been an unexpected gift. I realized now was the time to pay it forward. With help from my friend Ed, I was able to work out a deal with Apple. We made sure that Cody left that day with his very own phone. I've also continued to work with the NAPA Center. I'm proud to say that, to date, we've raised more than fifteen thousand dollars. To think, we went from a silly mission to get a new cell phone to having an opportunity to impact people's lives.

sgiving to Christmas Eve   mas Eve, the Postal   [See Shipping—

AL SEIB Los Angeles Times
APPLE, which has had success maintaining loyal customers, may not want to give out its phone number, but it has opened stores in many cities. Above, Internet personality Justine Ezarik rejoices over her new iPhone.

That video of my iPhone 6 adventure has since been viewed more than a million times and, as always, the reviews were mixed. Some people lamented the "relentless consumerism" or declared Apple enthusiasts nothing more than "sheeple." But that's okay. I'm okay with that, too.

Is it crazy to sleep on the street for two days, waiting in line to spend your hard-earned money on—of all things—a *phone*? Yes, it is. You know what else it was, though? It was *fun*.

We are surrounded by so many extraordinary things in this life that it's easy to become jaded. We carry around in our pockets and purses these unimaginable miracles of modern technology, these mind-blowingly powerful computers that allow us to speak—at a moment's notice—with anyone in the world, that grant us access to billions of pages of information; with the press of a button, we can read almost any book ever written, listen to any song ever recorded, or gaze into the face of a loved one, even if they are thousands of miles away. I think that's amazing. I don't want to be jaded. I want to marvel.

Is it silly to film yourself dancing like a spastic lunatic at thirty-five thousand feet in the air, flying somewhere over—I don't know, *Albuquerque*—trying not to slam into the elbows of cranky passengers who don't know who the hell you are? Yes, it is. You know what else it was, though? It was joyful. I mean, don't get me wrong—it was humiliating. But it was joyful.

We have so much in this life to worry about and suffer over that it's easy to become cynical—to not care too much about anything, because it's safer, cooler—but I'd rather be a bug-eyed, squealing enthusiast.

There are so many moments when we may feel judged or slighted or put upon or gossiped about, that it would be easy to lash out, to complain about all the ways in which we've been wronged, to point a finger at someone, to write a nasty anonymous comment to make ourselves feel better, but I'd rather be kind.

It's impossible to predict the ways in which the people we meet—online and off—will ultimately affect our lives, but I believe strongly that everything happens for a reason. *You* have been put into my life for a reason, and I have been put into yours. We may not know *why* yet, but I'm so happy that we've crossed paths.

Thank you for watching, and for reading.

ACKNOWLEDGMENTS

THERE ARE SO MANY PEOPLE THAT I WANT TO THANK THAT I WOULD NEED ANOTHER BOOK TO INCLUDE THEM ALL. Here is one HUGE THANK YOU to anyone I've ever met and everyone who has been mentioned among these pages.

To my entire family for putting up with my absolutely crazy antics—most of which aren't even in this book. You've always been so supportive of it all. Bre, thanks for being such a great sport when I bother you nonstop on camera (and your entire life growing up). Jenna, for sticking by my side on some of our craziest travel adventures (also, sorry our rooms were next to each other and you had to hear me play guitar until 3 a.m. every night). Mom and Dad for giving me the chance to figure out my dreams and for always being there for me. I love you!

To my grandma, you and Pap were my #1 fans from the start. You've always taught me to be myself and helped me find an outlet for my creativity. I love you and thank you for all your hard work you've put into the "iJ Chronicle Books." :)

Francesca Giaimo, first and foremost for being such an amazing, supportive friend, but also makeup artist/art director/producer/ sound/lighting expert, etc. :) Nathan Haugaard, for being so talented and shooting such fantastic photos throughout this book! Mike Krisza for design help with this cover . . . and a million other projects I always seem to throw at you last minute. Josh Sundquist for hanging out sometime and for giving me the confidence and inspiration to actually write a book. Cory ⚓. Ed + JB: Myspace, line camping and BFFs for life. I love you guys. Susie, all of our stories will be in the sequel. Steve, thanks for kicking me and allowing me to tell the story even though you don't remember it happening . . . clearly, it did. ;)

Petar Mandich, you're the real MVP!! Thanks for being the most amazing manager and best friend anyone could ever ask for (and also for carting twenty Macs to the cover photo shoot). To everyone at Addition and UTA for helping me reach new goals. To Thea Haigh for being one of my first big supporters—I'm beyond excited to be working with you and the Sunshine Sachs team! The biggest thanks and hugs to everyone at Keywords Press/Atria Books, especially my editor Sarah Cantin for always keeping us on track and Courtney Hargrave for taking my nonsense stories and helping turn them into an actual book.

To all the brands that I've had the pleasure of working with, thank you for trusting me to partner with you and make something awesome.

To all of my Internet friends: you are my true inspiration. Through the ups and downs you guys have always been there and have helped me through some of the toughest times, even those that I've never shared publicly. In your emails, tweets, and comments, I have read so many touching stories about how I've changed your life, but you have all done the same for me. For that, I cannot thank you enough.

To Pittsburgh—love yinz.